BUNNY BUNNY

ALSO BY ALAN ZWEIBEL

North

BUNNY BUNNY

Gilda Radner:
A Sort of Love Story

WRITTEN AND ILLUSTRATED
BY
ALAN ZWEIBEL

APPLAUSE
NEW YORK • LONDON

Bunny Bunny: Gilda Radner: A Sort of Love Story
by Alan Zweibel

Library of Congress Cataloging-In-Publication Data

LC Catalog # 97-71196

British Library Catalog in Publication Data

A catalogue record for this book is available from the British Library

APPLAUSE BOOKS
211 West 71st Street
New York, NY 10023
Phone (212) 496-7511
Fax: (212) 721-2856

A&C BLACK
Howard Road, Eaton Socon
Huntington, Cambs PE19 3EZ
Phone 0171-242 0946
Fax 0171-831 8478

Distributed in the U.K. and the European Union by A&C Black

First Applause Printing: 1997

Printed in Canada

This book was never meant to be read. At least not by strangers. Let me explain.

Writers are lucky. Whatever the mood, no matter the longing, the writer can use his words to connect himself to any world he wishes to visit. I happen to like my world very much: I am happily married, I have the three best children in existence and two loving parents. But I still miss my friend Gilda. A lot. So, in an attempt to connect, the lucky writer grabbed his pen and relived his most cherished memories of a relationship that, despite death, is still very much alive.

The words came easily. Sometimes early in the morning. Sometimes late, when everyone was sleeping. As the past came racing forward, I merely scribbled the dialogues playing in my head. It was exciting. It was funny. It was sad. It was innocently romantic. And it was personal. Very personal. The kind of thing that one keeps to himself.

But then I thought about the sense of loss that everyone, including those who never met Gilda, felt when she passed away. I wondered if, in addition to her work, there was something else that could pay appropriate tribute to Gilda's time on this planet. My thoughts, once again, were personal ones. Of the courage she displayed when she became ill. Of the emotional boosts she received when she needed them most.

Gilda's Club is a support community in New York City for cancer patients and their families that bears my friend's name. The moment I decided to donate the proceeds from this book to Gilda's Club, I started to feel more relaxed about having strangers read this. And to feel that these pages may even, in fact, be purposeful. But most of all I felt blessed that I once cared so much for someone that I can vividly describe the spirit I'm still imbued with five years after she died. It's like I said before, writers are lucky.

Alan Zweibel
LOS ANGELES, CALIFORNIA

BUNNY BUNNY

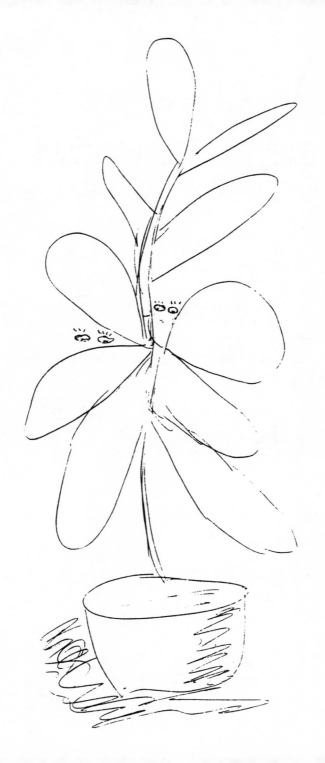

—Can you help me be a parakeet?

—Excuse me?

—I think it could be funny if I stood on a big perch and squished up my face, like this . . .

—Uh-huh . . .

— . . . but I need a writer to help me figure out what the parakeet should say. Could you help me?

—Really?

—Could you?

—Sure.

—Really?

—Yeah.

—Thanks.

—I'm flattered you asked me.

—You are?

—Uh-huh.

—Thanks.

—Don't mention it.

—I'm Gilda.

—I'm Alan.

—I know.

—How do you know?

—I took the liberty of asking one of the other writers if he knew the name of the big, nervous-looking guy who's trying to keep a low profile by sitting in the corner behind the huge potted tree, and he said your name was Alan. First job in TV?

—Yeah.

—It's a little overwhelming, isn't it?

—A bit.

—Just look at all the talent that's in this room.

—No, thanks.

—A producer who seems real smart . . .

—Uh-huh . . .

— . . . writers whose work I've admired for years . . .

—Me, too . . .

— . . . and a group of the funniest improvisational actors in the country.

—I know, Gilda.

—In two countries.

—Huh?

—Some of the actors are from Canada.

—Oh.

—It's scary.

—It's very scary.

—And that's why you're hiding behind that huge potted tree? Because you're scared?

—Yes.

—Because you're very scared?

—Yes.

—So am I.

—You are?

—Look, is it okay if I sit next to you behind that huge potted tree?

—Really?

—This is my first TV show, too.

—You're kidding.

—No I'm not.

—Wow.

—Well, can I?

—Can you what?

—Sit next to you.

—Sure, Gilda. Have a seat.

—Thanks.

—Comfortable?

—Sort of.

—Want me to move that branch away from the front of your face?

—No.

—Why not?

—Because this way we can keep talking but no one'll see our mouths move.

—That's true.

—I know.

—Plus, if either of us feels like fainting, we could get oxygen from these leaves.

—What do you mean?

—Photosynthesis.

—Photosynthesis?

—Remember? From school? Photosynthesis? The process by which green plants take carbon dioxide and, with the help of sunshine and chlorophyll, convert it to oxygen? Which they emit into the air? Which we breathe? Remember, Gilda?

—Yes.

—So what's your problem?

—This is an artificial tree.

— . . . I knew that.

—No you didn't.

—Did too.

—Yeah, right.

—And what if I didn't?

—Want some gum?

—Sure.

—What kind do you want?

—What kind do you have?

—All kinds of kinds.

—All kinds of kinds? What language is that?

—Here.

—What's this?

—My pocketbook.

—You're kidding.

—No.

—It's bigger than my high school.

—Take whatever you want.

—What are you talking about?

—The gum.

—It's in here?

—Help yourself.

—No.

—Why not?

—I can't.

—You said you wanted gum.

—I do.

—Then take some from my pocketbook.

—No.

—Why?

—Because you're a girl and I'm a boy and I might see things inside this pocketbook that will eventually be inside of you and that could be embarrassing considering that I'm a writer and I have a vivid imagination, so yes, I do want some gum but could you please serve it to me?

— . . . You're Jewish, aren't you?

—In a way.

—In a big way.

—I've seen bigger.

—Where? The Chabad Telethon?

—What's your point?

—That you're going to take some gum.

—No, I'm not.

—Bullshit you aren't!

—Ow!

—Take some gum!

—Stop pulling my hair!

—Open my pocketbook and take some goddamn gum!

—No!

—Yes!

—Ow!

—Take some!

—You're choking me!

—I know!

—I can't breathe!

—Get some oxygen from that fake tree, Jewboy!

—Very funny!

—Take some gum!

—No!

—Take it!

—Never!

— . . . Uh-oh.

—What's the matter?

—He's calling on you.

—Who is?

—Lorne.

—Oh, Christ.

—It's your turn to tell your ideas for sketches.

—Oh, Christ.

—Got any?

—Yeah, but . . .

—I'll handle it.

—What are you doing?

— . . . *Zweibel's got this great idea where I play a parakeet who at first has a lot of trouble learning how to talk so I just stand there with my face all squished up like this, but eventually I learn how to talk and don't stop talking until it gets to be so annoying that whoever plays my owner finally shuts me up by stapling me to my perch and gagging me with a shoelace and . . .*

—Psst . . . Gilda.

—What?

—Tell him that you'd like to play Howdy Doody's wife, Debby Doody.

— . . . *and Zweibel also has another funny idea where I play Howdy Doody's wife, Debby Doody . . . Yes, we're going to work on these and lots and lots of other ideas together . . . you know . . . like a team . . . Thank you.*

—Hey, everyone laughed.

—Debby Doody?

—Why not?

—Okay.

—Hey, Gilda?

—What?

—Thanks.
—Want a piece of gum?
—Yeah.
—Where you going?
—To buy some.

On a New York City Street That Night

— . . . and there's the Empire State Building . . .

—Uh-huh . . .

—St. Patrick's Cathedral . . .

—Right . . .

— . . . and you see that little guy who's selling pencils next to the subway?

—Yeah . . . ?

—That's Mayor Koch.

—Zweibel . . .

—I swear.

—Cut it out.

—Hey, ask any of these people. They'll tell you – it's his way of staying in touch with us commonfolk.

—Will you stop?

—Oh, you're just jealous because your mayor in Cleveland probably wouldn't think of a disguise like that.

—Detroit.

—Oh, like there's a difference.

—My dad died when I was fourteen.

—You were real close, weren't you?

—How could you tell?

—By the look on your face when you mentioned him.

—I miss him a lot.

—Sorry, Gil . . .

—He's the reason I became a performer.

—Really?

—Yeah, he loved performers. He owned a hotel in Detroit, but back in the thirties he somehow became friends with a few radio personalities.

—Like who?

—Gosden and Correll?

—The guys who played Amos and Andy on radio?

—They used to come over to our house all the time.

—Wow.

—Fibber McGee and Molly, too.

—You're kidding?

—No.

—God . . .

—They really made my dad laugh a lot.

—I'll bet.

—My dad used to love to laugh.

—Uh-huh.

—He was a quiet guy.

—Uh-huh.

—Sort of like you, Zweibel . . .

—Uh-huh.

—But better-looking.

—Oh.

—And when he'd laugh, his whole body would shake . . .

—Uh-huh.

— . . . and then everyone else in the room would start laughing . . .

—Right.

— . . . and then *their* bodies would start to shake.

—Wow.

—So, when I was a little girl, I'd try *my* best to make my dad shake. I'd tell him jokes or make up funny lyrics to show tunes or do impersonations of some of our goofier relatives . . .

—And he'd laugh?

—Yep.

—And shake?

—Like a leaf.

—That's great.

—What about yours?

—What about my what?

—Your family.

—What about them?

—What are they like?

—I don't know – just your typical middle-class, Long Island Jewish family who spend half their lives trying to figure out whose car they should take. Why are you laughing?

—I know that family.

—I had a feeling you'd understand.

—Oh, yeah.

—But I'm glad I have them.

—That's nice to hear.

—Family's always meant a lot to me, Gilda.

—Right . . .

—When I was a little boy, I used to watch the old *Dick Van Dyke Show* and say that that's the kind of life I want to have. You know, be a TV comedy writer, have a wife, a family, a home. That was my goal.

—And you're achieving it.

—The TV writer part, anyway.

—Are you seeing anyone, Zweibel?

—Well, sort of . . . not really . . . you know.

—Yeah.

—You do?

—Oh yeah. I just ended one of those "well, sort of . . . not really . . . you know" relationships.

—You did?

—Can you please get that waiter's attention?

— . . . sure. *Excuse me, sir?* Here he comes.

—Thanks.

—You want dessert, Gilda?

—No, I'm stuffed.

—*Anything else I can get for you two?*

—*Just a check, please.*

—*Very good.*

—*Oh, and sir?*

—*Yes, ma'am?*
—*Could I please have two cheeseburgers, a large fries and a vanilla shake to go?*
—*Absolutely.*
—*Thank you.*
— . . . Gilda?
—Yeah?
—I thought you said you weren't hungry.
—I'm not.
—Then who did you order that food for?
—Koch.
—Who?
—That little guy we saw selling pencils on our way over here.
—You're kidding.
—No.
—Wow.
—Wow?
—Yeah.
—What do you mean?
—You might be the nicest person I've ever met in my entire life.
—You just met me five hours ago, Zweibel.
—Okay, the third-nicest person.

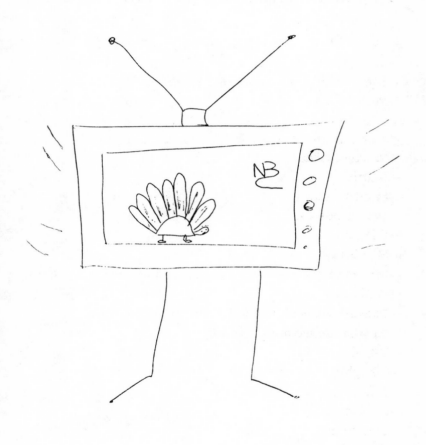

The First
Saturday Night Live

—Nervous, Gilda?
—A little.
—I understand.
—How about you?
—I'm okay.
—Horseshit.
—Nice mouth.
—Well . . . ?
—Okay, I'm scared, too.
—So what do we do?
—When?
—Tonight!
—Oh.
—Zweibel . . .
—Play to me.
—What do you mean?
—Gilda, when the show starts . . .
—Yeah . . . ?
— . . . and you're on the air . . .

—Live.

—Live . . .

—Oh, God.

— . . . try to make me laugh.

—You?

—Yeah.

—Why you?

—Well, there'll be a full audience in the studio and millions of people watching at home.

—I know.

—But I'll be standing right next to the camera you'll be playing to. Okay? So just make me laugh the way you did when we wrote the piece and I'm telling you that everyone else will laugh, too.

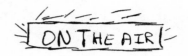

ON THE AIR

STUDIO 8H

After the Show

—Hello?
—Zweibel?
—Yeah.
—It's me, Gilda.
—Hi, Gilda.
—Hi, Zweibel.
—Gilda?
—Yes, Zweibel.
—What time is it?
—Four.
—O'clock?
—Yes.
—The 4:00 that's in the morning?
—That's the one.
—Wow.
—Zweibel?
—Yeah?
—You proud of me?
—Very.

—Really?

—You were wonderful on the show tonight.

—Really?

—You saw how much everyone was laughing.

—I saw *you* laughing.

—Well . . .

—I saw that big Mr. Potato Head of yours bobbing up and down next to that TV camera. And you know what? It made me feel good to see you there.

—Thanks, honey.

—And it also made me feel nervous that your big bobbing head might knock over the camera and that NBC would make you pay for it.

—Thanks, honey.

—And now comes the part where I ask how you liked the party after the show.

—It was great.

—Zweibel, can you believe all those people who showed up?

—Pretty amazing.

—All those actors and rock stars . . .

—And Dick Cavett.

—Mick Jagger, Paul Simon . . .

—Dick Cavett . . .

—What about Jack Nicholson?

—What about Catherine Deneuve?

—What about Catherine Deneuve's ass?

—What about it?

—Where was it? It wasn't at the party.

—Hmm . . .

—What are you thinking?

—That neither was Dick Cavett's.

— . . . Zweibel?

—Yeah?

—I met . . . "well, sort of . . . not really . . . you know."

—Uh-huh.

—She's really nice.

—I know.

—And cute.

—I know.

—Really cute.

—I know.

—And you know something, Zweibel?

—What?

—I'm really embarrassed to say this but, for a second . . .

—Yeah?

— . . . when I saw the two of you together . . .

—Uh-huh . . .

— . . . for a second I started to feel a little . . .

—Yeah?

—Are the two of you together right now?

—No.

—How come?

—We had a fight.

—Oh . . . ?

—Gilda?

—Yeah?

—Please complete that sentence.

—What sentence?

—You said you were starting "to feel a little" what?

—Look, I gotta go.

—Gilda . . .

—I'm serious. It's getting late and they want to close this place.

—What place?

—The restaurant.

—You're still at the party?

—What's left of it.

—Oh.

—Zweibel?

—Yeah?

—Call me tomorrow?

— . . . sure.

That Monday

—Zweibel, do you think this piece we wrote about Nadia Comaneci is offensive to Rumanian women?
—You mean the part where it says they have thicker beards than a lot of our early presidents?
—Uh-huh.
—I don't think so.
—Just checking.
— . . . Gilda?
—Yes.
—Who was that thin guy?
—What thin guy?
—Last night. That thin guy whose table you stopped at when we were leaving that restaurant.
—Oh, that was Eric . . .
—Uh-huh.
— . . . He was my boyfriend for a while when I lived in Toronto.
—Oh.
—God, was I crazy about him.

A Month Later

—Zweibel, are you losing weight?
—Who me?
—You really look thin. Have you been working out?
—A little.

Mail

—Hey Gilda, they gave me a MasterCard. Wow, this is great. Now I can buy a wallet.

—Listen to this: "Dear Gilda – I love you, I love you, I love you. I need you, I need you, I need you. I want you, I want you, I want you. I'll be out of here in three years. Please wait for me. Your fan, Stu."

— . . . Gilda?

—Yeah?

—Stu's going to be out of where in three years?

—Prison.

—You mean like jail? The slammer? The big house? The place where the warden talks into a megaphone when there's an uprising? That kind of prison?

—Yes, prison.

—Oh . . . prison. Well, here's an interesting question – are you scared?

—Of what?

—Gilda, the guy says he wants you and he's in prison. Aren't you even a little nervous that these two facts are in the same sentence?

—Not really.

—Oh . . .

—Stu's probably just lonely.

—Of course.

—You know what I mean?

—Absolutely – especially if he's been thrown in solitary for striking a guard . . . Hey Gilda, this is starting to be fun, isn't it? Fan mail, autographs . . .

—Yeah, my mom called from Detroit to tell me that I cost a contestant a lot of money on *The $25,000 Pyramid.*

—What do you mean?

—You know the show, right?

—Of course.

—Well, apparently the score was even so whoever won the tie-breaking round went on to play for $25,000.

—Right.

—Now the first contestant guessed all seven answers correctly, so the other contestant – this little old lady from Iowa who was playing with John Davidson – not only had to get all seven answers right, but now had to do it in less time than the first contestant.

—Keep going.

—Her category was famous comediennes, and she guessed the first six in like no time at all . . .

—Oh God . . .

—And then my name came on the screen.

—She didn't guess it?

—Didn't guess it? She and John Davidson just sat there and sat there in total silence and then they asked Dick Clark if maybe there was some mistake but Dick Clark said he wasn't sure so he had to ask the judges and before you knew it the time was up and the little old lady didn't win the money she was going to use to fix her husband's truck.

—Gilda, that's a terrible story.

—I know.

—And your mother called to tell you this?

—Four times.

—Jesus, we must have the same mother. You hungry?

—Yeah.

—Want to go out and break in my new MasterCard?

—Give me a few minutes.

—Sure. What are you doing?

—Writing a note to that little old lady.

—You're kidding?

—No. I called the *Pyramid* show and they gave me her name.

Central Park

—The trees really look pretty, don't they?

—Quit changing the subject.

—You know, I've never been to Detroit. Do your leaves also change colors or is that just an East Coast thing?

—Zweibel . . .

—I don't know what you want me to say.

—I just want you to be honest about this whole thing.

—Honest?

—Come on.

—Okay . . .

—Well? Do you love her?

—I did. A lot.

—But what about now?

— . . . I don't think so. At least I don't feel it.

—So end it.

—It's more complicated than that, Gilda.

—How?

—It's been three years. We've been through a lot. She traveled with me to the hotels when I was selling jokes to those Catskill comics, and stayed out till all hours when I started hanging out at the clubs. And now that I'm finally making a living, there's no more excuses about not committing, but I just can't.

—So end it.

—But it's hard to break up after all this. I keep asking myself what kind of person does a thing like that?

—An incredible shitheel.

—That was actually meant to be a rhetorical question.

—Sorry, but a lot of people will think you're an asshole . . .

—I know.

— . . . but you can't keep this thing going for the wrong reason. It's not fair. To her or you.

—I know.

—So end it. Deal with the guilt. Remember the good times and move on.

—It hurts. A lot.

—No one said it doesn't. Christ, I've been through it a thousand times myself.

—You have?

—Are you kidding? Every time my relationship with a guy ends, I'm usually such a basket case that I always promise myself I'll never get involved again.

—To spare yourself the pain.

—Uh-huh.

—That's understandable.

—Sure it is. But it's also stupid to not get a dog because it's going to die someday.

— . . . Run that by me one more time.

—You buy a dog, right?

—Right.

—And unless it's a stuffed dog, one way or another it's eventually going to die, right?

—Right . . .

—So what are you supposed to do? Deprive yourself of all that love and fun and affection because one day you're going to be sad? That's dumb.

—That's smart.

—What's smart?

—What you just said. That whole dead-dog thing.

—You think so?

—Yeah, it makes a lot of sense.

—But, Zweibel . . . ?

—Uh-oh . . .

—You know what also makes sense?

—What?

—That once the dog is dead you bury it.

—Not necessarily. Isn't there an expression about letting dead dogs lie?

—Those are sleeping dogs.

—Damn.

Her Apartment

—Hi.

—Zweibel . . . ?

—Hi.

—What are you doing here?

—I did it, Gilda.

—Did what? Why are you so out of breath? What are you doing here?

—It was the hardest thing in the world to do, but I took your advice and I ended it. It's over. I buried the dead dog. Do you believe it? I buried the dead dog and then I ran all the way down here to tell you.

—Zweibel . . .

—Can I come in?

—*Gilda?*

—Hey, who's that?

—Zweibel . . .

—Oh God, it's a guy. Oh God, you're on a date. Oh God, I should've called. Oh God, he's not wearing a shirt.

The Next Day

—I'm sorry, Gilda.
—It's okay.
—Then you're not mad at me?
—No, I'm not mad at you.
—Sure?
—Sure.
—Then why aren't we talking?
—Because we're in a movie theater and the movie is on.
—See? You are mad at me.
—Why do you say that?
—Because if you weren't, we wouldn't be at a movie so we could be talking.
—But you're the one who suggested we go to a movie in the first place.
—That's because I thought you were mad and didn't want to talk.
—I'm not mad.
—Sure?
—Zweibel . . .

—Sorry.

—Okay.

—It's just that . . . oh, here comes the part where Michael finds out that it was Fredo who betrayed him.

—Thanks.

—Sorry . . . it's just that I've been feeling vulnerable lately, and you and I have been spending a lot of time together, and maybe I've been thinking about you more than I should and I really didn't mean to embarrass you in front of that guy who didn't have his shirt on but . . .

—Zweibel?

—Yeah?

— . . . I love you.

—Excuse me?

—You heard me. I love you. But it scares me, and I don't want to talk about it, so can you please shut up and watch the fucking movie?

— . . . Nice mouth.

The
Long Island Rail Road

— . . . and we have a such a good thing going work-wise that I don't think we should rush into anything too quickly. . . .

—Uh-huh.

— . . . you know what I mean, Zweibel?

—Uh-huh.

—And don't you agree?

—Well . . .

—Plus, let's not forget that both of us aren't real good at staying friends with people after we break up with them so let's not be stupid, okay?

—Okay.

—Let's just follow these new feelings we have for each other . . .

—Okay.

— . . . and slowly see where they take us, okay?

—Okay.

—But slowly, okay?

—Okay.

—With no pressure . . .

—Okay.

— . . . and no rules.

—Okay.

— . . . except that we're going to take it slowly.

—Gilda . . .

—Yes.

—Can I remind you that we're on a train to my parents' house? Not Plato's Retreat. Not the South of France. But my parents' house. Now I can't even imagine a slower beginning to a relationship – but if it makes you feel better, and I mean this sincerely, I'd be more than happy to go back to Penn Station and check my penis into a locker.

—Very funny.

—I'm serious. They have that special penis-storage section behind Track 24.

—Okay, okay, I'll change the subject. What else should I know about your family?

—Well, my father manufactures jewelry and, for some reason, my mom says "Port of Authority."

—Port *of* Authority?

—Yep.

—You mean where the buses live?

—That's the Port.

—But why Port *of* Authority?

—It's baffled us for years. Then again, when my grandmother used to want a cold drink she'd ask for a "glass iced tea" – so maybe this is my mom's way of giving back. Uh-oh . . .

—What's the matter?

—Richard Carlton.

—Who?

—That guy coming up the aisle.

—What about him?

—I hate him.

—Why do you hate Richard Carlton?

—Because he's a schmuck.

—Why is Richard Carlton a schmuck?

—Because he kept bugging me in high school . . .

—Yeah?

— . . . and because when I moved back in with my parents after college, he kept making fun of me because I wasn't making any money writing and he had his own apartment because he was working in a stupid bank.

—He made fun of you?

—Yeah, with that dumb smirk and moronic giggle of his.

—That son of a bitch.

—I hate him.

—So do I.

—You don't even know him.

—Kiss me.

—What?

—We'll show that bastard.

—Gilda . . .

—Kiss me.

—Like this?

—Hey, you kiss pretty good.

—Well, I'm a man.

—*Alan?*

—*Oh, hello, Richard.*

—*What have you been up to, Alan?*

—*Well . . .*

—*Still working in the deli and trying to be a writer?*

—*Well . . .*

—Aren't you going to introduce me, darling?

—Darling? Oh, I'm sorry . . . *Richard, this is Gilda.* And Gilda, this is . . .

—*Gilda? From TV?*

—*Oh, hello, Richard.*

—*Boy, I'm a big fan of yours.*

—*Why, thank you, Richard. However, I do believe that your kind words are a tad misdirected.*

—Jesus . . .

—*What do you mean, Gilda?*

—*Well, like any other actor or actress, I'm only as good as my writer.*

—*Him?*

—*Absolutely. But then I doubt that comes as any surprise to you, Richard. Alan tells me you went to high school together, so I'm sure his talents were obvious to you even back then.*

—Jesus . . .

—*Oh yeah . . . yeah, Gilda. They sure were . . .*

—Jesus . . .

—*. . . I've always been a big fan of Alan's brand of humor.*

—*I know. It's really silly and quirky and that's just part of the reason I love him so much.*

—*Oh, you and Alan are . . . a . . . you know?*

—*Yes, but we're taking things slowly.*

—Jesus.

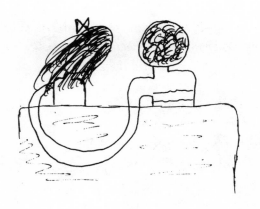

The Return Trip

—I owe you, Gilda.

—No you don't.

—Yes I do.

—Hey, I really like your parents . . .

—I owe you.

— . . . and their neighbors . . .

—I owe you.

— . . . and all those shopkeepers that your mom introduced me to when we went to buy cake . . .

—Oh, God . . .

— . . . at that mall that didn't have a bakery.

—Oh, God . . .

—But that all worked out just fine because when that couple that your mom hasn't seen in five years because she can't stand how they're always bragging about how well their son is doing unexpectedly dropped by during dessert . . .

—Hy and Rhoda Rappaport?

— . . . *they* brought a cake.

—Gilda?

—Yes?

—I owe you.

Studio 54

—Okay Gilda, we're even.

—What do you mean?

—You know exactly what I mean. I said that I owed you, and you paid me back, so now we're even.

—Did it make you laugh?

—A lot.

—Really?

—Oh come on. I'm walking around Studio 54 at a party given for you and the other cast members of the show and there's loud music and strobe lights and all kinds of disco stuff and out of the corner of my eye I see my mother dancing with Halston and my father trying to look down Bianca Jagger's dress and how can I help but laugh? When did you invite them?

—The day after we had dinner at their house.

—It's really funny.

—I thought I'd surprise you.

—That you did.

—And did you see the Rappaports?

—What are you talking about?

—Hy and Rhoda. The people whose asses your mom loves to shove your success up. There they are.

—No . . .

—See? In the corner? The couple who's showing pictures of their children to Andy Warhol?

—Oh man . . .

—And Zweibel?

—What now?

—See what's next to them? On the bar?

—Gilda?

—Yes?

—Is that a cake box?

—Uh-huh.

—You actually had the Rappaports bring a cake to Studio 54?

—Uh-huh.

—Gilda?

—Yes?

—I love you. A lot.

Travel Plans

—Hey Gilda, they gave me a Visa card. Wow, this is great. Now I can pay my MasterCard bill.

—Zweibel?

—Yeah?

—You think we're doing the right thing going away together?

—When are we going away together?

—Christmas. To the Bahamas. Aren't you nervous?

—No.

—Why not?

—Because six other people from the show are also going, and we're all staying in separate rooms, and since the travel agent screwed up, you and I aren't even on the same flight. So I'm not sure that this trip technically falls into the "we're going away together" category.

—Oh.

—Feel better?

—Yes, thank you.

—I'm here to help.

Paradise Island

—You look cute in a bathing suit.

—Thanks, Zweibel.

— . . . Well?

—Okay, you do, too.

—Why, thank you, Gilda.

—The beach is nice, isn't it? White sand, the water's real blue . . .

—The whole island's beautiful. You know, maybe we should rent a motorcycle at that place next to the hotel and do a little exploring, huh? . . . What's so funny? Oh, me on a motorcycle?

—No.

—What then?

—You wearing a motorcycle helmet.

—I understand.

—Oh, did I hurt your feelings?

—She asks while still laughing.

—I'm sorry. It's just that . . .

— . . . that I'm a fairly large guy with a very large head? I know. I own a mirror. I just wish I had a dollar for every time

I've been told I look like Woody Allen with a glandular condition.

—I would've thought you'd be flattered by that.

—Why?

—Isn't Woody Allen your idol?

—As a creative force, absolutely. But physically I would have preferred the James Caan/Sonny Corleone/"Okay, I'll do you a favor and let you sleep with me"–type look.

—Oh, I see.

—You know the look?

—I used to date a guy like that.

—And?

—It was great.

—I hate you.

—Really great.

—Jesus, why don't you just draw me a picture and hit me over my huge head with it.

—Okay, I'll stop.

—I appreciate it.

— . . . Zweibel?

—Yeah?

—Is the Freddie Prinze thing still bothering you?

—I guess so.

—Want to talk about it?

—What can I say? We weren't real close. I just knew him from the clubs. Sold him a few jokes. Years ago . . .

—Uh-huh.

—But still the thought of a twenty-two-year-old kid who's got the world by the balls killing himself is pretty scary.

—I never met him but it made me cry.

—I know what you mean.

—Did you hear those stories about Freddy's agents at his funeral?

—You mean how they were hustling to get their clients to be pallbearers so they'd be on TV and get the publicity?

—Yeah.

—It's a weird business at times. Have you noticed that, Gilda? It's as if all the values and rules about decency our parents made the effort to teach us don't apply.

—Yeah, but couldn't you say that about any business?

—I guess you could. I really wouldn't know – this is the first business I've ever been in. Then again, maybe it's success in general that's confusing. You know, one day not having anything, and the next day you can have everything. I know *my* head's spinning a little. Nine months ago I was slicing meat in a deli and now . . . Did you know that American Express makes you pay the whole balance at the end of the month?

Table for Six

—Gilda, isn't Paradise Island great?
—Yeah, it's really great, Marilyn.
—Alan, isn't this restaurant great?
—Yeah, it's really great, Marilyn.
—Gilda, you got burned today.
—Thank you, Neil.
—So did you, Alan.
—Thank you, Neil.
—Gilda, how's your room?
—Oh, it's great, Tom.
—Alan, how's yours?
—Oh, it's great, Tom.
—Hi, I'm Kokoba, and I'll be your waiter for the . . .
— . . . Gilda.
—What?
—They're on to us.
—What do you mean?
—Shh! Whisper. Kokobar might be wearing a wire.
—What do you mean they're on to us?

—I think they know we're not sleeping together . . . yet.

—What do you mean . . . "yet"?

—Yet. You know, as in . . . "yet."

—As in "we haven't but we eventually will"?

—Exactly . . . Right? . . . Hello?

—*Did you hear that, Gilda?*

—*What?*

—*Did you hear that, Alan?*

—*What?*

—*Kokoba says that this restaurant's been used in a few James Bond movies.*

—*You're kidding? Is that right, Kokobar?*

— . . . Zweibel?

—What?

—It's Kokoba.

—What did I say?

—Kokobar.

—It's not Kokobar?

—No, it's Kokoba.

—Kokoba.

—Right.

—Without the "r."

—Right.

—Kokoba.

—There you go.

—Gilda?

—Yes?

—This is a stupid conversation.

—Hey, we're on vacation.

In the Casino

—I don't believe you! I really don't!

—Gilda . . .

—Why the hell did you do that?

—Gilda . . .

—Zweibel, will you please tell me why you picked up the check at dinner?

—Sure . . .

—And why you found it necessary to give Kokoba an 80% tip?

—I'd be happy to tell you.

—Well?

—I needed the cash.

—What?

—You heard me. I was low on cash and the restaurant took Diners Club, so I figured I'd put it on my credit card, everyone would pay me back with cash and I'd have some money to gamble with.

—Zweibel?

—Yes, honey?

—Have you ever gambled before?

—No, but I've been watching that special channel on the TV in my room that teaches you how to play blackjack.

—Jesus . . .

—Not to worry.

An Hour Later

—Gilda!

—Jesus, I've been looking all over for you.

—Gilda, look!

—What?

—Look! Money! I won!

—You what?

—Look! $1,100!

—How the hell did you do that?

—Blackjack.

—You're kidding.

—Nope.

—Good going, Zweibel. That's great.

—Where were you?

—Over there. Playing the slot machines with everyone else.

—How'd you do?

—I lost.

—Is that a fact?

—Oh, stop gloating like a big asshole.

—I'm not gloating.

—Yes you are.

—I know. Hey, what are you doing now?

—I'm going upstairs.

—You are?

—Yeah, I'm really tired.

—Then could you do me a favor?

—What?

—Well, I'd like to be somewhat mature about the $1,100 I won. There're a lot of bills I can make minimum payments on with this money.

—So?

—So I'm going to give you $1,000 of it and I want you to hold on to it until we're off this island.

—You sure?

—Very sure. I don't even want to know about the money until we're out of here.

—Fine. But I want you to understand that I'm going upstairs to my room.

—I understand.

—Because I'm real tired . . .

—You've had a very hard day.

— . . . and I'm going to sleep.

—You'd be a fool not to.

—No kidding around, Zweibel.

—I'm not kidding around.

—So give me the $1,000 . . .

—Okay.

— . . . and that leaves you with $100 to gamble with.

—More than enough.

—And the deal is that if you lose this money . . .

—Couldn't happen.

— . . . you can go fuck yourself . . .

—Also couldn't happen.

— . . . because I'm going to sleep.

—As you should.

—Good night, Zweibel.

—Good night, Gilda.

Five Minutes Later

—Gilda?
—Get lost, Zweibel.
—Gilda, honey?
—Go back downstairs.
—Could you please open your door?
—We made a deal.
—Gilda . . .
—Go away.
—Gilda, I have to tell you something.
—Let me guess – you lost the $100?
—Well, yeah . . .
—And you want me to give you more money?
—Well, yeah . . .
—Zweibel?
—Yes?
—Go fuck yourself.
—Now look, Gilda, you're a terrific friend to keep the money
from me and I really appreciate it . . .
—Go away.

— . . . but it *is* my money that I want.

—What about your minimum payments?

—All I want is a hundred more dollars.

—Sorry.

—What are *you* sorry about?

—That I'd rather burn the money than let you gamble it away.

—Come on.

—No.

—Gilda!

—No, you'll hate me in the morning.

—Big deal, I hate you now. Now come on.

—No.

—Gilda!

—No!

—What gives you the right?

—You gave me the right.

—So now I'm taking back that right.

—Indian giver.

—Gilda.

—No.

—Gilda!

—Keep your voice down.

—Then open the door.

—I can't.

—Bullshit.

—I'm serious. Kokoba and I are dancing naked with your money and he gets embarrassed. "Don't you, Kokoba?" "Oh yes, my lovely Gilda."

—Bad impersonation.

—Then go away so I can work on it.

—No.

—Okay, then go up and down the elevator till morning.

—No.

—Then I don't know what to tell you.

—Gilda!

—Stop yelling.

—Gilda!

—And stop pounding on my door like that. Who are you, Fred Flintstone? Get it? "Pretty funny, huh, Kokoba?" "Oh yes, a regular laugh riot, my lovely American Gilda. Now let us dance the dance of the Zweibel money."

—Gilda!

—How's that impersonation?

—It's getting worse.

—And so are you. Go away.

—Gilda!

—Scram.

—Gilda!

—You're not going to stop, are you?

—No, I don't plan on it.

—Well, then . . . okay.

—What do you mean?

—You're a huge pain in my ass, Zweibel.

—I know.

—And I really shouldn't do this.

—But . . . ?

—I'll be right there.

—Really?

—Yeah. Just give me a second.

—Sure.

—But don't go away, okay?

—Okay . . . Look, Gilda, I'm real sorry about this outburst. I really am. It was just so frustrating. I was playing 21 and I had 20 but then the dealer got 21 and I don't know how much you know about gambling but, believe me, the odds of such a thing happening are very, very slim . . . Hey, hurry up, all right? The casino closes in an hour and I really want to get down there and kick some butt . . . Boy, you're a good friend. Watching out for me and my money like this. But trust me, I know what I'm doing . . . Gilda? The weirdest thing. These two Bahamian security guards – you know, the ones who wear those white safari helmets and carry those large wooden clubs – just got off the elevator and they look like they're looking for someone . . . Wow, they're coming this way . . . Jesus, they're pointing . . . and shouting . . . at me. Dammit Gilda, I can't believe you called the cops on me . . . you cow!

—Don't worry, I'll hold on to your money, Zweibel.

The Flight Home

—Mr. Zweibel?

—Yes?

—Go to the bathroom.

—Excuse me?

—You are Alan Zweibel, seat 7B, correct?

—Correct.

—Then please go to the bathroom.

—May I ask why?

—Please, sir . . .

—Well, with all due respect – and trust me, I think you're an amazing stewardess for being this thorough – but I really don't have to go to the bathroom.

—Yes, you do.

—Oh . . . Look, just so I know, do I smell like I have to go to the bathroom?

—No.

—Is there something I'm doing that's prompting the other passengers to turn on their overhead nozzles?

—No, it's nothing like that.

—Then what is it?

—Look, all I know is that about an hour before we boarded, this girl . . .

—Girl?

— . . . this adorable girl with these real sad eyes came up to me and told me how nervous she was that her friend might be mad at her because she called the cops on him and since she was on a different flight back to New York she handed me an envelope that had a note she'd written to him and asked if I'd do her a favor and tape it behind one of the toilets on the plane because he wouldn't be mad anymore once she made him laugh and toilets make Zweibel laugh because you're not very mature.

—And you did her the favor?

—Yes.

—That's very nice of you.

—Are you still mad at her?

—I'm not mad.

—Good.

—And thank you for helping out.

—My pleasure. You know, I'm a big fan of your friend's but I really didn't recognize her at first. But once she started talking I was so touched by how warm and funny and loving this person was that I felt like I knew her my whole life and would've done anything for her. Isn't that odd? By the way, it's the lavatory on the left.

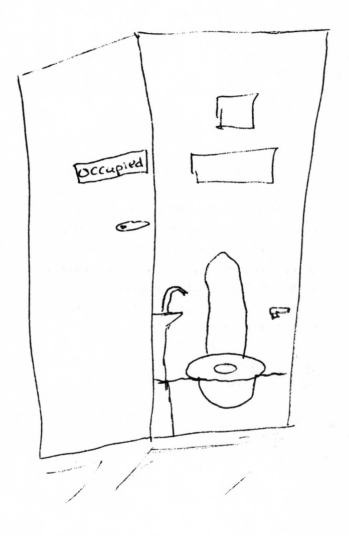

In the Lavatory on the Left

Dear Zweibel,

Sorry about last night but I had a job to do and you were such an asswipe. Anyway, now you're in the air and here's your stupid money—all $690 of it. Yeah, I know you gave me $1,000 but I decided I would hold on to the $310 you laid out for everyone's dinner and will give it back to you when your next Diners Club bill comes, so you won't be tempted to spend it on something you probably don't need before then.

Gilda

P.S. Call me when I get home.

Fans at a Knicks Game

—Hey, Gilda!

—Hello.

—Hi, Gilda.

—Hello.

—Hey Gilda, can you sign this?

—Sure.

—Then me?

—Sure.

—Then me?

—Sure.

—Hey Gilda, you're really funny.

—Thank you.

—Hey Gilda, you're really pretty.

—Thank you.

—Hey Gilda, you're my favorite.

—Thank you.

—Hey Gilda, my birthday's also in June.

—Oh, really?

—Hey Gilda, I also used to be real fat.

—*Oh, really?*

—*Hey Gilda, I also have trouble keeping a boyfriend.*

—*Oh, really?*

—*Hey Gilda, who's that goofy-looking guy with the "I Love New York" hat who keeps trying to put his arm around you?*

—*Oh, that's Zweibel.*

Halftime at the Knicks Game

—Excuse me, but did you happen to notice where the girl who was sitting here went?

—Are you Zweibel?

—Yeah.

—Gilda said to tell you that she's down there.

—Oh God . . .

In a Cab
After the Knicks Game

—You mad?

—No, Gilda.

—Angry?

—No, Gilda.

—Perturbed?

—No, Gilda.

—Then what are you?

—I'm not sure.

—But you are something?

—Oh yeah.

—Zweibel . . .

—Alright, let's figure this one out together, okay?

—Okay.

—Fine. We go to a basketball game, right?

—Right.

—We have these great seats, down by the court, and you're recognized by lots of people, right?

—Right.

—But I'm okay with that.

—You sure?

—Gilda, I'm real proud of everything that's happening to you . . .

—Really?

—Oh, come on, I'm nuts about you. And it makes me feel great when I see people embrace you the way they do. They should.

—Thanks . . .

—So I don't have a problem with that at all.

—But . . . ?

—But what I don't understand is how, in the few short minutes it took me to go get us snacks, how you not only got to meet the players who've been my idols since I entered puberty . . .

—They introduced themselves to me . . .

— . . . but how you got to sit next to them on the bench . . .

—They invited me . . .

— . . . while I get tackled by every security guard in America when I try to get down there to hand you your delicious popcorn.

—I'm sorry.

—By the way, have you noticed lately that every time I try to get near you, the cops come? Why is that?

—I said I'm sorry.

—There's nothing to be sorry about. It was just a little embarrassing, that's all. I've never been booed by 19,000 people before. You hungry?

—Zweibel?

—Yeah?

—Could you do me a favor?

—Sure.

—I mean a real big favor.

—What?

—Promise you won't get upset?

—Never.

—Or hurt?

—Uh-oh . . .

—Because I mean this in a good way.

—What, Gilda?

—Could you please not call me Gilda anymore?

—Excuse me?

—I mean it.

—Why don't you want me to call you Gilda anymore?

—Because everybody does.

—Well, isn't that your name?

—I'm scared, Zweibel. I'm real excited about what's happening to me. It's what I'm working for, and it's what I've always wanted and I'm grateful and it's fun but I don't trust it. It's a weird feeling having strangers call me by my name and knowing all sorts of things about my life that I never told them. So it would make me feel better if you didn't call me what everyone else did.

—Sure.

—Thanks.

—Gilda?

—Yeah?

—Any thoughts about what I should call you?

— . . . Gilbert.

—Gilbert?

—Yeah.

—Makes perfect sense to me.

Hiatus

—Hey Gilbert, it's me. Look, I'm calling because I figured that since we have some time off from the show that maybe we can hang out a little or maybe go to a movie or see *Beatlemania* or work on some characters for you or whatever. But, you're not home, so . . . give me a call when you get this message . . . Bye.

☎

—Hi, Gilbert. It's me. I just heard your message – I completely forgot that you're doing all those interviews this week. I hope they're going well. Look, Gilbert, I'm not sure but you might be getting a call from a man called Mr. Omerza who's a lawyer from Carte Blanche and who's angry at me because of my bill. Well, today he was yelling at me and then one thing led to another and I told him that I knew you and then he stopped screaming because he's a fan but he didn't fully believe me so I gave him your number and if he calls please tell him that I'm a good guy and not to worry because I always pay *you* back whenever you lend me money. Thanks.

☎

—Hey Gilbert, it's me. Sorry I missed your call again. I'm glad the interviews went well but it's too bad you couldn't make it tonight because we're having a lot of fun. First, we all went to see *The Bad News Bears* because Walter Matthau's hosting the show next week and we're thinking of maybe doing a parody. And then we piled into a cab and went to Uncle Thai's – you know, that Chinese restaurant on Third Avenue – which is where I'm calling you from right now and it's really great. Everyone's real loose and relaxed and full of all kinds of ideas for sketches for our next batch of shows. I actually came up with a few of my own – one in particular where you'd play a nosey matron who works in the ladies' room at a posh hotel and knows all the gossip and weird bathroom habits of celebrities and the social elite – which I thought was pretty funny but no one else did, except for this really cute Chinese waitress who laughed a lot when I ran it by her . . . Look, I better get back to the table so I'll speak to you later or see you at work tomorrow. Bye.

The Next Day

—I feel bad, Gilbert. Real bad. I feel like I cheated on you.
—You mean because you porked the Chinese waitress who thought your nosey-matron sketch was funny?
—It just happened. We all finished dinner, we all went home, then I came back to the restaurant, waited until she was done with her work, walked her home, and it just happened.
—Well, I don't know what to say except don't feel bad.
—No?
—No.
—Oh . . . Why?
—Why shouldn't you feel bad?
—Yeah.
—Because I don't.
—You don't?
—No.
—Oh . . . Why?
—Why don't I feel bad?
—Yeah.
—Do you want me to feel bad?

—Yes.

—Oh, really?

—Very, very bad. In fact, I was hoping that you'd feel just awful. There was even a small part of my brain that was hoping you'd smack me.

—And what would that prove?

—That you and I had a real relationship.

—But we do.

—Oh, come on, not really.

—Look Zweibel, when we first met we made a pact . . .

—*You* made a pact.

—Okay, I made it. And I stand by it.

—But it's not natural. We say we love each other and we spend so much time together and not only do I think it's un-natural I also think that we may even be breaking one of the Ten Commandments or even one of the laws of gravity at this point.

—I agree.

—You do?

—I think it's very unnatural . . .

—So?

— . . . and that's why I think you and I should slow things down a little bit more.

—Slow things down? If we go any slower my penis will be in reverse. Just what are you saying?

—I'm saying that besides the great work we do together, I need you in my life because I trust you more than anyone and I don't want to lose that.

—Why would you lose it?

—Don't you see that we're both going through so many changes and we're both so confused that right now the only way we can help each other and get through this together is by downplaying the boy-girl part of our friendship? At least for the time being. That's the only way we can be sure that you and I are going to last.

—So you're saying that, for the time being, I should date more Chinese waitresses.

—Zweibel?

—What?

—I spent time with someone this weekend, too.

—You did?

—Yeah.

—A guy?

—Yes, a guy.

—Oh . . .

—Nothing special, but . . .

—Did he call you Gilbert?

—No.

—Did you call him Zweibel?

—No.

—Well, I'm glad about that.

—His name is Jack, and he's very nice, and if he asks me out again I'll probably say no, and if he doesn't call again it'll break my heart and that's where I am right now and I refuse to bring that craziness to us. Do you understand?

—Yeah. I understand.

—And does what I'm saying make sense to you?

—Yeah, it does.

—Good. So do you think you can live with these new rules?

— . . . Sure.

Passing in a Hallway

—Hi, Zweibel.

—

—

—

—

—Oh, hello, Gilda.

—Are you alright?

—

—

—

—

—Just fine, thank you.

—

—

—O-o-o-kay. Well, I gotta go.

—

—

—

—

—Yeah, me too.

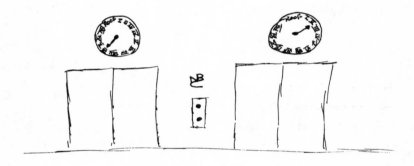

—Hold the elevator! Thank you . . . oh . . .

—Hello, Zweibel.

— . . . Hello.

—

—

—

—

—

—

—

—

—

—You okay with this whole Three Mile Island thing?

—I'm just fine, Gilda.

—

—

—

—

—

—

—

—

—

—

—

—Bye, Zweibel.

—Bye.

Thoughts in a Bobbing Head

—What a jerk I am. What a big, stupid, Jewish jerk. Just look at me, for God's sake. Standing next to this camera, my huge head bouncing rhythmically to the cadence of her dialogue as if things haven't changed between us. They have, though. I hate her. I hate her very, very much . . . But she *is* funny. Much funnier than the words I stayed up until 4:00 this morning writing for her. Boy, does the audience love her. Whether she puts on a wig and a funny accent or dances across this studio floor with Steve Martin, they just love her . . . Well, that's their problem because I hate her. I truly, truly do. Even more than Hitler.

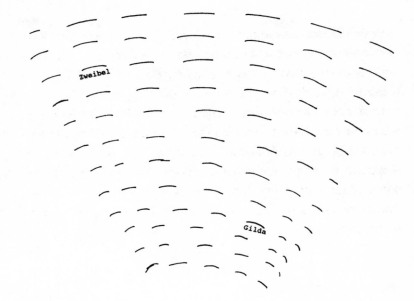

Extremely Lonely
in a Pittsburgh Hotel Room

—How long have you been writing?

—I don't know. For a while, I guess.

—Wow, that's neat.

—Well . . .

—That's really, really, really, really, really, really neat.

—Thank you.

—You're so very welcome.

—And how long have you been a hostess in the restaurant downstairs?

—Three months.

—And before that?

—What do you mean?

—Well, what did you do before you became a hostess in the restaurant downstairs?

—Oh, I was a hostess.

—Excuse me?

—But not downstairs. Upstairs. This hotel also has a restaurant on the roof and I worked there until I got promoted to the restaurant in the lobby.

—Oh, I see. You worked on the roof before you got kicked upstairs to the lobby.

—What do you mean?

—Oh . . . well . . . kicked upstairs is another way of saying promoted.

—Really, Alan?

—Trust me.

—So that was a joke?

—I thought so . . .

—You know, I just realized that I'm an extremely lucky, lucky, lucky hostess.

—Really?

—Because if I weren't, I wouldn't have been kicked up the stairs and then I wouldn't have met you when you were eating breakfast with all your college buddies this morning.

—Uh-huh.

—Are those guys all here for the wedding, too?

—Yeah. Our friend Dave . . .

—Is Dave the fat one?

—No, the guy we were calling Buddha is the fat one.

—Oh . . .

—Anyway, Dave went to medical school here in Pittsburgh and this is where his fiancée is from so all the guys flew in from wherever they were to be here.

—That's so nice.

—Yeah, it's like a reunion.

—Are any of your friends also writers?

—No, just me.

—What do they do?

—Well, Dave's a surgeon and Roy's a . . .

—Is Roy the fat one?

— . . . No, Buddha's the fat one.

—Oh, right.

—So like I was saying, Roy's a psychologist . . .

—Wow, he must be smart . . . Alan?

—Yes, Darleen?

—Do you think I'll get along with all your friends at the wedding tonight?

—Sure. Everyone's real friendly . . .

—Wow, it sounds super neat.

—Yep, it will definitely be super neat.

—Alan, are you the only one of your college friends who isn't married?

—Ah, no. Buddha's also not married . . .

—And which one is Buddha, again?

— . . . The fat one.

—Oh, right.

—Right . . .

—Buddha's the fat one, Buddha's the fat one. Got it.

—Right . . . Look, does this hotel have a florist shop?

—You mean one that sells flowers?

—Yeah.

—There's one in the lobby.

—Thanks.

—Where you going?

—I'll be right back.

Back at Work

—Zweibel!

—What?

—Don't give me "what."

—Huh?

—Why the hell did you send me flowers from Pittsburgh?

—I sent you flowers from Pittsburgh?

—First you don't talk to me for six weeks, you snub me like I don't exist or like I committed some crime, you don't even write for me anymore unless Lorne forces you to—and then, out of the clear blue, you send me flowers from Pittsburgh? Why?

—Well, I was at the wedding of an old friend and my date was a hostess in a restaurant on Mars and I was lonely . . . I'm sorry. I didn't mean to upset you.

— . . . I'm not upset.

—Really?

—Really.

—I'm glad . . . How did you know they were from me, anyway? I didn't enclose a card.

—I called FTD and they told me it was you.

—Oh.

—My neighbor said they were pretty.

—Your neighbor?

—Yeah. I didn't get to see them.

—What do you mean?

—I wasn't home this weekend but apparently the delivery boy left the flowers at my door. So my neighbor down the hall, who's this gay guy, saw the flowers and knew I was away and didn't want them to go to waste so he gave them to his boyfriend who he was having a fight with.

—So what you're saying is that I sent a gay guy flowers?

—Well, not really . . .

—Gilda?

—Yes?

—What you're saying is that I sent a gay guy roses from Pittsburgh.

—Well, in a roundabout way maybe you did.

—Jesus . . .

Flowers from Pittsburgh

Later at a Coffee Shop

—I miss you . . .

—I miss you too, Gilbert.

—And I'm worried about you.

—You are?

—Yes.

—Why?

—Because I know you've been doing drugs.

—Me?

—Cut the shit, Zweibel. You're doing cocaine and that's real dangerous for anyone who's as naturally insecure and paranoid as you.

—How do you know? Did someone tell you? Does everyone know?

—I don't know if anyone else knows. But just because you and I've been having a tough time doesn't mean that I haven't been paying attention. I see what's going on and I'm telling you that you don't have to resort to that shit.

—Okay.

—Don't give me "okay." That stuff plays weird games with

your personality and you're a good guy who's been acting like an asshole because of it.

—I have?

—Yes.

—To who?

—To everyone.

—Oh.

—But in particular to Robin.

—Who?

—Robin Blankman.

—Who?

—The production assistant you've been dating secretly – but I can tell because I see you look at her the same way you used to look at me.

—You think I've been an asshole to Robin Blankman?

—Ahhh, so you know who I'm talking about.

—Yeah. Now what about her?

—She's terrific. Robin Blankman's beautiful, she's smart, she loves you, and if you lose her because you're fucking around the way you are, I'm personally going to slit your throat.

—You are?

—From ear to ear.

—Why?

—Because I care about you.

—You do?

—Go to hell.

—Okay, okay – but what about you?

—Don't worry about me.

—But I do.

—Don't.

—Don't?

—I'm a big girl.

—I know.

—I can take care of myself, alright?

—Fine.

—Good.

—So how are things between you and Brad?

—He moved out.

—He did?

—Yeah.

—Oh . . . sorry . . . You alright . . . ?

—No.

—Anything I can do to help?

—Just start looking me in the eye again . . . okay?

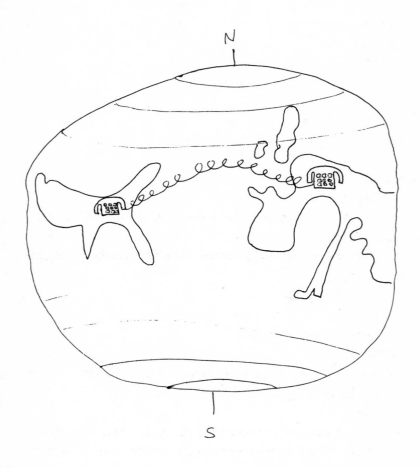

Long Distance

—Hello.

—Zweibel?

—Hey Gilbert! It's great to hear your voice! Did you buy me a present?

—You're the one who's in Europe. Shouldn't you be buying me something?

—Yeah, I forgot.

—So how do you like it there? Having fun?

—Yeah. London was great . . .

—Uh-huh.

—I was there for ten days working with the Monty Python guys, who all asked me to say hi to you . . .

—Hello.

— . . . and since they knew that this is my first trip abroad, they took me all over and showed me everything and guess what . . . ?

—You met George and Ringo.

—How the hell did you guess that?

—Zweibel, you called me at 2:00 in the morning from a pay phone in the nightclub to tell me.

—Yeah, but you weren't home.

—I know, but then you called my mother in Detroit and told her and then she called and told me.

—Oh, that's right. I forgot.

—But it sounds like it was fun.

—It was. Except that when the script was finished all the Python guys took off in different directions and I started to get real lonely real fast.

—That's what my brother said.

—Oh yeah, I called him from the airport when your mother's line was busy.

—Uh-huh . . .

—You know, she should really get call waiting.

—I'll tell her.

—So now I'm here alone in Amsterdam where yesterday, I'm sorry to say, I might've hit my all-time low socially.

—What'd you do?

—I tried to pick up a girl at Anne Frank's house.

—Run that by me one more time.

—It was pathetic. I was on this tour . . .

—Oh God . . .

— . . . and everyone was quiet and real sad and there were these pictures of Anne and her family and we saw the attic where they hid and I started getting a little overly sentimental so I told this cute girl that I had an Emmy and that I was pretty sure that *The Diary of Anne Frank* was playing on the movie channel back at my hotel.

—Jesus . . .

—I know.

—Did she go back to your hotel with you?

—No, and neither did her very muscular Nordic boyfriend who I didn't realize was also on our little tour.

—Well, maybe they had other plans.

—Yeah, probably – which now brings us to the Robin Blankman part of this conversation.

—Why?

—Because I called her this morning.

—You did?

—Yeah, I called her in New York and asked her if she'd meet me in Paris.

—And . . . ?

—And she said yes.

—That's great!

—You really think so?

—Come on. You know how I feel about that girl.

—I know.

—So what's the matter?

—I'm a little nervous about it, okay?

—Good.

—Gee, thanks.

—I'm serious. That means you really care about her and might even be ready to get serious about your feelings.

—You say that like it's a good thing.

—It is, you idiot . . .

—Oh . . .

— . . . and you know it.

—Hey, I was just kidding around. I write jokes for a living, remember?

—Yeah, and when you get back I want to talk to you about that.

—What do you mean?

—It can wait.

—Yeah, but now I can't wait.

—Zweibel, you're on vacation.

—Oh, like I'm really going to relax now that you've opened this little can of worms.

—It's just a little idea I've been toying around with . . .

—Right . . .

—That I might want to put together a one-woman show . . .

—Really?

—On Broadway . . .

—Wow.

—But it's just a thought and it wouldn't happen until next summer so we have time to talk about it.

—Okay.

—Besides, I'm having too much fun right now to even really think about work.

—You are?

—That's right.

—A guy?

—Uh-huh . . .

—What's his name?

—None of your business.

—Oh . . .

—But he's really great and . . .

—Where'd you meet him?

—None of your business.

—Oh . . .

—But he's really terrific and who knows, if things continue like this, I may not even be interested in doing a show next summer.

—Has he seen you naked?

—None of your business.

—Well, have you seen him naked?

—Jesus . . .

—Just answer one of those naked questions, okay? Because let's face it, if you've seen him naked then he's probably seen you because I can't imagine any situation, with the possible exception of doing laundry, where only one person . . .

—Zweibel . . .

—What?

—You get naked when you do your laundry?

— . . . Sometimes.

—Why?

—Why not?

—Boy, you've really changed since you've been to Anne Frank's house.

—Most people do.

Labor Day

—It was the most romantic time I've ever had when I was with another person.

—That's great, Zweibel.

—We had this terrific room in a small hotel in Paris, where every morning we'd have tea and croissants . . .

—*Cwois*sants.

—What?

—You pronounce the "r" like a "w."

—Oh. Rell, anyway, we would then explore the city and at night we'd take walks along the Seine and we never ran out of things to talk about and it was so relaxing to be away from the pressures of script deadlines and ringing phones and all that.

—And then you guys drove to the South of France . . .

—How do you know that?

—I spoke to Robin Blankman.

—You did?

—Yeah, she told me that you guys rented a car and slowly worked your way down to Nice.

—Right . . .

—And that when you were in Nice you spent a lot of time on the beach gawking at the European women walking around with no tops on.

—Well . . .

—But when some old man just happened to glance in Robin's direction while she was removing her wet top and putting on a T-shirt, you gallantly defended her honor by screaming at the man and then throwing his eyeglasses into the Mediterranean.

—Robin told you about that?

—Oh yeah.

—Great.

—So? What's the deal with you two?

—With me and Robin Blankman?

—Yeah.

—I really like her.

—That's great.

—Hey, I'm not looking to settle down just yet . . . .

—But . . .

— . . . but I do want to keep seeing her exclusively and, if I'm lucky, maybe ten, fifteen years will go by before she starts pressing me to make a commitment.

—Jesus . . .

—I'm kidding.

—I hope so.

—Hey, how are *you* doing?

—Fine.

—You look pretty, Gilbert.

—Thanks.

—What's the matter?

—Nothing.

—Bullshit. What's going on?

—I'm becoming a cliché.

—How so?

—You know, one of those show business clichés who's popular with strangers but has no personal life.

—But you were real happy when I spoke to you from Europe.

—I know.

—You're not with that guy anymore?

—No.

—What happened?

—He left.

—Why?

—I told him to.

—Oh . . . how come?

—He didn't take me seriously.

—In what way?

—Look, it's probably just as much my fault as his. People tell me that I confuse guys, and maybe I do. They see me one way, but then they get to know me and they're disappointed. But you know me, Zweibel. I have enough trouble being strong for myself, let alone for someone who gets paranoid when I'm quiet or gets threatened when I say "Bunny Bunny."

—When you say . . . ?

—"Bunny Bunny."

—What's that?

—Oh, nothing, really . . .

—Tell me.

—It's silly.

—Tell me.

—When I was a little girl . . .

— . . . Go ahead.

—When I was a little girl, I used to be afraid of the dark. We lived in this big house and at night there'd be these scary shadows on my bedroom walls. So, what I'd do, was get under the covers and say the words "Bunny Bunny" to protect me from the shadows while I was sleeping.

—Why "Bunny Bunny"?

—I'm not sure. I really don't remember. Except that it worked. The bad dreams stopped. And then, when I started getting older, I cut back and only had to say it once a week and, finally, once a month – just to be on the safe side.

—I understand. It's not silly. You were a kid and you . . .

—I still say it.

—You do?

—Yeah. Maybe it's a habit or a superstition or . . . I don't know. It's just that, for whatever reason, on the first day of every month the first words that I say when I wake up are "Bunny Bunny" to make sure it's going to be a good month and keep me safe from anything bad that could happen.

—Like what?

—I don't know. Everything. Does that sound stupid?

—No.

—But I'm in my thirties.

—So?

—And it still doesn't sound stupid?

—Gilbert, everyone has their own little . . .

—If Robin Blankman did something like that, would you make jokes and put her down for it?

—Is that what this guy did?

—Without a letup.

—Even after you explained what it meant to you?

—Yeah.

—What an asshole.

—But you still haven't answered my question.

—You mean would I feel insecure if Robin said something other than my name when she first woke up?

—Yeah, would you go crazy?

—Well, those are two different questions. Yes, I'd feel insecure, but I don't know if eating twelve bags of potato chips and then shooting my brains out counts as going crazy.

—I forgot who I was talking to.

Valentine's Day

—Zweibel, you're an idiot.

—I know.

—I can't believe how stupid you are.

—I know.

—Why did you do it?

—I don't know.

—Why in God's name did you ask both your *and* Robin Blankman's mothers to be in a sketch on the show?

—Well, here was the thought . . .

—I can't wait to hear this logic.

—Robin and I have been getting along real good . . .

—Right . . .

—But our families had never met. So, since Robin and I are both Jewish . . .

—You thought it'd be a good idea to cast them as extras in a Bar Mitzvah sketch?

—Yeah.

—With Kirk Douglas playing the Bar Mitzvah boy's grandfather?

—I thought it would be fun.

—Really. And now what do you think?

—Gilbert, I had no idea that it was going to turn into such a bloodbath.

—You didn't?

—That they were going to hate each other at first sight? No. That one mother would bolt from rehearsal because her table in the Bar Mitzvah sketch wasn't as close to Kirk Douglas's table as the other mother's table? No. And that it would take everybody in the studio, including Spartacus himself, to break up the catfight after one mother made that remark about the other mother's closeup looking like her dog's ass on a hot day? No. No way in hell. Why are you laughing?

—Well, think how weird it was for me – just sitting there in my dressing room when out of the corner of my eye I see all hell breaking loose on my monitor.

—It was on the monitors?

—Zweibel, it was a camera rehearsal. At a television network. Remember?

—You mean other people might've seen the fight, too?

—Might've? That picture was fed to every monitor in the building.

—Oh no . . .

—I heard John Chancellor talking about it in the commissary.

—Oh God . . .

—And I know at one point it was on all of the TV screens in the NBC family store.

—You mean tourists buying mugs with peacocks on them saw it?

—Uh-huh.

—Oh, God, no . . .

—How's Robin dealing with all this?

—She's pissed at me.

—She is?

—Well, she's embarrassed. Here we were, trying our best to keep our relationship low-key and dignified, and now you're telling me that this fiasco was beamed to our troops overseas.

—You want me to speak to Robin for you? Maybe I can cool her off a little.

—What would you say?

—That you meant well . . .

—Okay.

— . . . and that you're an idiot.

—Good, because she tends to forget.

In a Seafood Restaurant

—It'll be called *Gilda Live.*
—Uh-huh . . .
—And it'll be a one-woman show where I'll get to play a lot of my characters . . .
—Right . . .
—And we'll start rehearsals in June . . .
—Okay . . .
—And it'll open on Broadway in August . . .
—Wow . . .
—And I want to know if you'd like to write for it?
—Of course.
—Really?
—What kind of question is that, Gilda? I'd be honored to be one of the writers for your show. It'll be fun.
—It'll be hard work.
—Okay.
—It will be a lot of very hard, very intense, very serious work.
—Okay.
—Oh, we'll have some fun, but we're going to work hard.

—Gilda . . . ?

—Yeah?

—Will we be doing a show or building a highway?

—I'm sorry, Zweibel. But I've decided to take charge of my career and, if you don't mind me saying, I suggest you start doing the same.

—What do you mean?

—I mean you should watch your flank.

—My flank?

—That's right.

—What's wrong with my flank?

—I think you should protect it.

—I should protect my flank? Is somebody planning to attack it?

—I'm just saying that if you don't protect it, nobody else will.

—What in God's name are you yapping about, Gilda?

—Look, you see what's happening. People from the cast are starting to do movies and have success on their own. Away from the group, and away from our show. And that's what I would like to do.

—Uh-huh . . .

—I would like to start getting my own identity and to try doing different things . . .

—Uh-huh . . .

— . . . away from everyone else.

—I understand.

—You do?

—Absolutely.

—Zweibel . . . ?

—Yeah?

—Do I sound bitchy or horrible when I talk like this?

—No.

—Really?

—Not at all.

—Thanks for being so understanding.

—You're welcome.

—And for letting me have space while I'm going through some changes . . .

—You're my friend, Gilbert.

—I know . . .

—And I would do anything for you.

—Thanks.

—Just one question, though.

—Yeah?

—What does all this have to do with my flank?

—Jesus, we're back to your flank?

—What did you hear? What do you know?

—Listen to me, you moron . . .

—Come on, I'm a big boy. I can take it. Should I clean out my desk?

— . . . The Germans.

—What about the Germans?

—The Germans are going to attack your flank.

—Cut it out.

—But I think you're going to be okay because historically their armies tend to show mercy on big boys with clean desks.

—Why are you doing this to me?

—Because you're annoying as all hell.

—Oh?

—All I'm saying is that the show has been wonderful to you, too. It's earned you respect in the industry and maybe now's a good time for *you* to start branching out a little. You know, making inroads in movies and in the theater and . . . what's the matter? What's going on with your face? I've never seen it that color. These are compliments I'm giving you. You're a good writer. Why are you crying? Dammit, Zweibel, I've got so many problems of my own and I really need you to be strong for me but first you've got to be strong for yourself and you . . . Jesus, what's happening to your face? Your lips are the size of inner tubes!

In an Emergency Room
Two Hours Later

—It was the oysters.

—The oysters?

—Yeah, the doctor said that I'm allergic to shellfish and it was those twenty-seven oysters I ate that made me blow up like that guy in the Michelin ads.

—But you eat oysters all the time, Zweibel.

—Well, apparently there are some allergies that you can acquire later in life and shellfish is one of them.

—Your swelling's gone down.

—Yeah, they gave me a shot and a half of Benadryl and that seems to be doing the trick.

—A shot and a half?

—Well, the doctor started laughing at me in the middle of the first shot and the needle broke.

—God, you did look weird.

—I know.

—Who I really felt bad for was Eduardo Ruiz.

—Who?

—The cab driver who drove us here from the restaurant.

—Really?

—Well, yeah. We were in his backseat, with me holding your ever-growing head, and at one point he actually asked me to tilt you onto your side because he couldn't see out his rearview mirror, and then he started crying.

—We'll have to send him something.

—I tipped him $50.

—Good girl . . . Gilbert?

—Yeah?

—Thanks.

—For what?

—For tonight. Thanks for dinner, and for asking me to help write your Broadway show, and for taking care of me when my lips blew up, and for tolerating my insecure ramblings about my job being in trouble.

—You're welcome.

—I really appreciate it, Gilbert.

—I know.

—Especially that part about my job. In fact, I'm a little embarrassed about the way I behaved.

—Don't worry about it.

—I don't know what came over me.

—Forget it.

—It must've been the shellfish talking.

—Probably.

—But, once again, I'm really sorry.

—Okay.

—You're not mad?

—No.

—I'm glad . . . really glad . . . Gilbert?

—Yeah . . . ?

—Look, just for my own peace of mind, can I ask you one last very, very quick question? Just to finish up that conversation we were having about my job?

—Okay.

—Just a very, very quick question.

—Sure.

—Great.

—But on one condition.

—What?

—That afterwards we go back to the restaurant and you eat a very, very large lobster.

—No.

—Then shut the hell up.

—Fine.

The Winter Garden Theater

—Gilda . . . ?

—This is amazing . . .

—Is everything okay? I was sitting in my seat, waiting for your show to start, when one of the ushers said you wanted to see me backstage.

—I want to show you something.

—What are you looking at?

—Okay, now just part the curtain, like this, and look out at the audience and tell me what you see.

—Well, I see a full house . . .

—Right . . .

—Mostly regulation people but also some celebrities like Barbra Streisand and John Travolta and Glenn Close and . . .

—Check out the middle section, about halfway up.

—I see some of the other writers . . .

—Two rows behind them . . .

—I see my family, I see my seat, I see Robin, and I see Robin's family . . .

—Which consists of . . . ?

—Robin's sister, her father, her mother, and her mother's hair.

—Exactly. Now look at the seat behind Robin's mother's hair. Who do you see?

—No one. All I see is hair.

—Keep looking.

—Oh, wait a second, you're right. There is someone back there. Some guy whose head is moving from side to side like he's trying to peek around the bouffant to get a clear view of the stage.

—That's what I thought.

—Poor guy. It's like getting a seat behind the foul pole at Yankee Stadium.

—Can you make out who that poor guy is?

—No.

—Well, it's Rex Reed.

—Rex Reed?

—Yep. He's here to review my show for the *Daily News.*

—While he's swinging back and forth? God, he looks like a windshield wiper with a sports jacket. How's he going to take notes?

—Well, what choice does he have? It's a matter of simple arithmetic. I'd say Rex Reed is around 5′7″ and when he's sitting he's probably around 4′5″. On the other hand, Robin's mother's around 5′5″ when she's standing but after she's had her hair done she's still around 5′5″ when she's sitting. So unless someone runs out and buys Rex a periscope . . .

—Or a Weedwacker . . .

—*Two minutes, Gilda.*

—*Thanks, Peter.*

—Look, Gilda, I'll just go back and have Robin's mom change her seat.

—I'm not so sure that's a good idea . . .

—I'll have her switch with Robin's father . . .

—I don't think so.

—Or I'll just send her to a movie.

—I appreciate it, Zweibel, but I think we should leave it the way it is. Remember the last time we tried to move her seat? It almost made the sports pages.

—Yeah, but that was about Kirk Douglas.

—I know.

—This is Rex Reed. We're talking about a completely different species.

—No, leave it alone.

—You sure?

—It will be fine.

—Okay. Then, Gilda . . . ?

—Yeah?

—Why'd you want me to come back here?

—*One minute, Gilda.*

—*Thanks, Peter.*

—How come?

—Because I wanted to thank you. And I wanted to tell you that I love you and that I'm happy for you.

—What do you mean?

—You know what I mean.

—No I don't. Especially that "I'm happy for you" part. You know how remarks like that always throw me.

—You and Robin. I think it's great.

—What do you know? What do you think you know? Who the hell told you?

—*Ready, Gilda?*

—*Ready, Peter.*

On the Phone — Later

—No one had to tell me, Zweibel.

—Really?

—Absolutely. I was peering out at you guys and noticed that Robin never looked prettier and that you never looked whiter and I just knew you were engaged.

—Well, obviously you were the first person we wanted to tell but we wanted to wait until after your opening when things were less hectic. But hey, great news – even though we're getting married, Robin said it was okay for you to come live with us so we can still play.

—Thank you.

—You're welcome.

—Is Robin with you? I'd like to congratulate her and extend my condolences at the same time.

—No, she's at her apartment . . .

—Oh.

—Hopefully putting together her dowry.

—Hopefully . . .

— . . . Gilbert?

—Yeah?

—Good going tonight.

—You really think so?

—Oh, come on. You got three standing ovations. Twelve if you count all the times Rex Reed stood so he could see over Mt. Saint Hair. You were terrific.

—Thanks.

—Fifteen hundred people in the theater and then the crowd afterwards at Sardi's, everyone was there for you . . .

—Did you see the drawing Hirschfeld did of me?

—Yep.

—Pretty neat, huh?

—It was terrific. Everything was. You did real good.

—But you know what the strangest thing was, Zweibel?

—What?

—When I was on the stage performing . . .

—Yeah . . . ?

—I couldn't see anyone.

—What do you mean?

—The audience. Once the show started, the lights shining on me were so bright that I couldn't see a thing.

—You're kidding.

—No. It was like I was shouting jokes into a cave and then people in the cave were laughing back at me.

—God . . .

—So you know what I did?

—What?

—Since I couldn't see anyone?

—What?

—I pictured my father and I made believe he was the audience.

—You did?

—Yeah . . .

—Was he laughing and shaking?

—Yeah, he was.

—It was a great night, Gilbert. It was a great, great night.

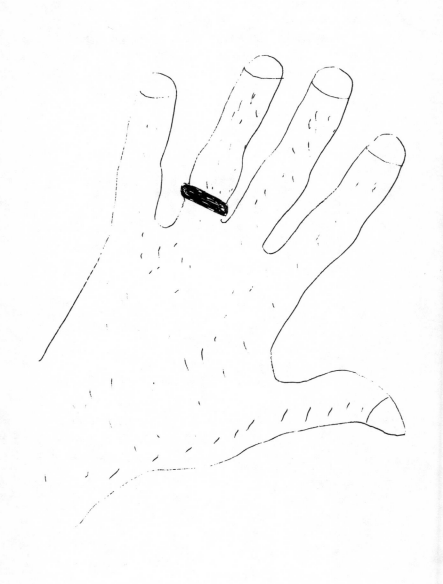

On the Phone —
Three Months Later

—It was a ridiculous night. I'm just sorry you weren't there, Gilbert. Then you could've seen for yourself just how absurd the whole thing was.

—What happened?

—Well, first of all, you should know that Robin and I were more than respectful of the fact that our parents were throwing this wedding . . .

—Uh-huh . . .

—It was a big night for both of our families so we stepped aside and left the planning totally in their hands and figured that unless Kirk Douglas just happened to be at Temple Beth Shalom in Livingston, New Jersey, that night, there'd be no problems with things like seating arrangements and all would be fine between our families.

—Right.

—But we were wrong.

—Kirk Douglas *was* at the temple?

—No.

—Then what was the problem?

—Well, apparently Long Island and New Jersey have different rules concerning who pays for what at weddings. But our folks never discussed that part and just assumed that their own rules applied.

—Oh no . . .

—So, we had no flowers and two bands.

—You did not.

—Gilda, it was a battle between the Dave Elgart Trio and the Jackie Sheldon Experience.

—No . . .

—So we heard every song twice.

—No . . .

— . . . and the best man was called upon to make two toasts.

—No . . .

— . . . and Robin's Uncle Marvin had a heart attack dancing his second limbo.

—Get out of here . . .

—Gilda, I swear on Robin's Uncle Marvin's blue lips that all this happened.

—Did Robin's Uncle Marvin die?

—No, but when they were wheeling Marvin out, one of the paramedics grabbed some food, so our parents had an argument over whose guest he was because no one wanted to have to pay the caterer for what he ate.

—This is astounding . . .

—Afterwards, Robin and I checked into the Hotel Pierre and hid under the bed for the rest of the night.

—I don't blame you . . .

—Robin's still under there.

—And what about your honeymoon?

—We leave tomorrow.

—For Puerto Rico?

—Don't make fun. I was told it's very, very beautiful there.

—By who?

—My travel agent . . . Consuela Espinosa.

—Jesus . . .

—Look, we had to choose a place that wasn't too far away because we all have to be back at work next Monday.

—Oh, that's right.

—Will you be back by then?

—Yeah. I have a matinee on Sunday and then I go straight to the airport.

—How are the shows going? How's Chicago?

—The shows are going great . . .

—Are the audiences laughing the hardest at my stuff?

—No.

—Oh. Well, then is the audience silently acknowledging my stuff to be the most witty and Noël Cowardesque?

—No.

—Oh.

—But I do have a new boyfriend.

—You do?

—Yep.

—Anyone I know?

—I doubt it.

—Why do you doubt it?

—He's a musician.

—Hey, I know musicians. I had fifty of them at my wedding. Which one is he?

—He's the bass player in my show.

—Oh, I know him. He plays that guitar that runs on electricity, right?

—That's the one.

—He's a great guy.

—I really like him, Zweibel. And we're talking about living together.

—That's great, Gilbert. And don't worry, your secret's more than safe with me.

—What secret?

—About your new boyfriend.

—It's not a secret.

—Oh . . . then I can tell people?

—Sure.

—Great.

—But people already know.

—Oh . . . how many people know?

—I don't know. We've been on the road.

—So your band knows?

—Yeah.

—And the crew?

—Yeah.

—How about people here in New York?

—Well, maybe. I imagine people might've made calls and said something to their friends or . . .

—How about Puerto Rico?

—What?

—Do people in Puerto Rico know that you have a new boy-friend?

—I doubt it.

—So I'll tell *them*.

—I appreciate your covering that for me.

—You're welcome.

Newlyweds

—Zweibel?

—Hey, Gilda.

—What are you doing?

—Watching *Family Feud.* It's a good one.

—Can you tape it and watch it later?

—This is a tape. What's up?

—I'm sending a cab to come get you.

—What for?

—None of your business.

—Oh.

—Is Robin around?

—No. She's out furniture shopping.

—Then you'll come by yourself.

—Where to?

—None of your business.

—Oh.

—When the cab gets there in about fifteen minutes, just get inside of it.

—And what do I say to the driver?

—Don't say anything.

—Oh.

—He already knows what to do with you.

—Which is?

—None . . .

— . . . "of your goddamn business, you whiny, oversized, ego-maniacal pain-in-the-ass"?

—Just get in the cab, alright?

In a Big Government Building – Later

—I can't believe I'm married.

—Congratulations, Gilbert.

—Can you believe it? Can you believe that I'm actually married?

—Sure.

—You can?

—Well, a cab comes and picks me up at my apartment, it then stops at the Dakota to get the two of you, then it drives us down to City Hall, where some man sitting behind a desk asks you a bunch of questions in a room with a big flag. The way I see it, either you're married or the three of us just had our driver's licenses renewed.

—Oh, look how cute my brand-new husband looks paying that court clerk over there . . . It's weird, isn't it, Zweibel?

—What is?

—That you and I are both married now.

—Yeah, but it's fun. Robin and I are having a lot of fun.

—She's been looking great.

—Well, it's been three months now and . . .

—How are things between her and your mom? Any better?

—Not really.

—Why?

—Well, personally I think my mother's still upset that I didn't marry one of my sisters. But I'm real excited for you, Gilbert. I've never seen you glow like this before.

—Well, I'm in love and I'm happy and I finally have a family. I mean a real family. You know, show business has all these false families that trick you because people spend a lot of time together and are real close and then, when the production is over, everyone scatters right after the wrap party.

—I know.

—And that wrap party could be soon if those rumors about Lorne and all of us not coming back to the show after this season are true.

— . . . Oh.

—What's wrong?

—Even the fat guy?

—What fat guy?

—The fat guy. With the ponytail? The one who has all those tattoos? You know, the one who's missing a thumb?

—You mean the fat guy who sets up the doughnuts in our studio?

—Yeah.

—What about him?

—I'm not going to see him again after the wrap party?

—No.

—Damn.

The Last Show — May 1980

—Our last show. It's hard to believe. This is the last time that I'll be standing next to this camera with my head bobbing while she makes everyone laugh. It's real strange. Right now I'm a part of something that's so alive. And so vital. And so safe. But starting tomorrow . . . ? God, I'm scared.

At the Wrap Party

—Alan?
—Yes?
—Hi!
—Uh . . . hi.
—You don't recognize me, do you?
—Ah . . .
—Blue.
—Blue?
—It's me! Blue! The guy who sets up the doughnuts in the studio!
—Oh . . . hi . . . Blue.
—Hey, don't feel bad. A lot of folks don't recognize me since I shaved off my ponytail.
—Not to mention the rest of your hair.
—I just felt it was shedding time again. You know the feeling.
—I do?
—'Course you do. According to Gilda over there, you've been known to shave your head more than once or twice yourself.
—Gilda, huh?

—Yeah, she says that you and me have a bunch in common and that you were nervous that we'll lose touch 'cause you're leaving the show so here's my phone number and address out at the trailer park. You and your bride should come up and visit me and my ol' lady sometime.

—Gilda, huh?

—She's a real cutie. Me and the rest of the crew are sure gonna miss her.

—Yeah, I know . . .

—Say, she tells me you enjoy working on a lathe.

—Excuse me?

—Yeah, when I told her that's how I lost my thumb, on a lathe, she said that's another thing you 'n' me have in common 'cause you have your own woodshop where you make your own furniture but that she's worried 'cause, no matter how many times she reminds you, you still sometimes forget to wear goggles and Alan, that's how I lost this eye . . .

—Oh, no . . .

—See?

—Oh, God . . .

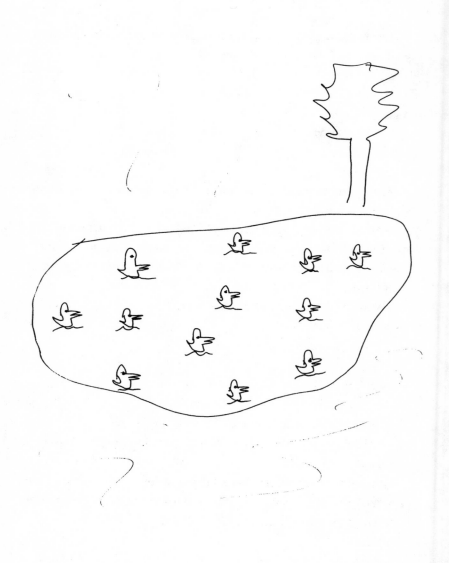

— . . . It's a play called *Lunch Hour.*

—Uh-huh.

—Written by Jean Kerr.

—Right . . .

—And it'll be directed by Mike Nichols.

—Jesus, Gilda . . .

—Yeah, it's pretty exciting.

—I'll say.

—Let's walk this way.

—Boy, Gilbert, this place is beautiful.

—Did you see everything?

—I think so. Robin and I took a walk before the barbecue started.

—Did you see the very, very large garden?

—We saw the very, very large garden, and the very, very green greenhouse and . . . Oh my God.

—What?

—Gilda, what are those?

—What are what?

—Those things that are swimming in that very, very wet pond. Jesus, Gilda, those are ducks.

—I know.

—Gilda, you have ducks.

—Well, not really. I just rent this summer house. They sure are cute though, huh?

—Very cute. They're very, very cute rented ducks.

— . . . So, how are you, Zweibel?

—I'm fine.

—Bullshit.

—I'm not fine?

—Oh, I think you're fine. I think you're doing great. Problem is, *you* don't think so.

—You've been talking to Robin, haven't you?

—Yep.

—Wonderful . . .

—She says that you haven't been sleeping.

—Look . . .

—Because you're worried about making a living.

—I really feel funny talking about this.

—You know, it's only a matter of time until things start falling into place for you and your career starts moving forward again.

—I know.

—You do?

—Not really.

—It will . . .

—By the way, did Robin also tell you that she's pregnant?

—Is she?

—We found out yesterday.

—Wow . . .

—Pretty astonishing, huh?

—Were you guys trying?

—I know *I* was.

—I'm sure you were.

—Though, for a while, there was a question or two about my sperm count so I had to go to a doctor who handed me a special jar and charged me $150 to go into the bathroom and do what I've been doing for free since I was thirteen . . . okay, four.

—That would've been my guess.

—Thanks.

—Hey, do your parents know that Robin's pregnant yet?

—You want to hear what happened?

—Uh-oh . . .

—Yeah, this is a beauty. Robin and I were sitting home last night and, oh, first of all you should know that we had already called both sets of parents earlier and told them the good news.

—Okay . . .

—And I thought we handled it well, quite frankly. After the doctor confirmed that Robin was pregnant, we didn't want to offend anyone, so first we called my parents and said, "Mom, Dad – we want you to be the very first to know that we're going to have a baby." And then we called Robin's parents and told them the same exact thing.

—Not a bad move.

—I thought so. But then last night we're watching TV and the phone rings and it's my mother, who said that she and my father want to buy the furniture for the baby's nursery. So I thanked her and I hung up and told Robin that my parents were buying the nursery furniture and then the color drained from her face because it seems that her parents had called earlier and said the same thing.

—That they were buying the furniture.

—Yep, and this is a problem for us because they're all acting as if this is a big honor and God knows that we don't want any more bloodshed.

—So what are you going to do?

—What choice do we have? We'll just set up two nurseries and move the baby from one to the other depending on which set of grandparents are over.

—Jesus . . .

—Unless you have a better suggestion.

—Oh, no. I'm not going near this one.

—I don't blame you.

— . . . Zweibel?

—Yeah?

—Congratulations about almost becoming a father.

—Thanks, Gilbert.

—Excited?

—Very.

—Scared?

—Shitless.

A Monday Night — December 8, 1980

—Hello.

—Zweibel . . .

—Gilda?

—Zweibel . . .

—Gilda, are you okay?

—Zweibel . . .

—What's wrong? Why are you crying?

—Didn't you hear?

—Hear what?

—Someone shot John Lennon . . .

—Oh my God . . .

—Right outside the Dakota . . .

—Why would anyone want to shoot . . . ?

—He's dead . . .

—Gilda?

—What?

—Where are you?

—In my apartment. Zweibel, some sick son of a bitch assassinated John Lennon a hundred feet from my front door and now there's tons of people outside singing Beatles songs and . . .

—You want us to come over?

—Yeah, but you shouldn't.

—Why not?

—Because it's freezing outside and Robin is pregnant and I doubt that the police will even let anyone who doesn't live here into the building.

—Okay, but it sounds like we should talk.

—Call me later.

—I feel like everyone's childhood ended tonight.

—I know . . .

—I mean it, Zweibel. This wasn't political or anything like that. We're talking about the Beatles and peace and "Love Me Do" and *The Ed Sullivan Show*.

—And Shea Stadium . . .

—Uh-huh . . .

—Remember when they played there?

—Sure I do. And, whenever I hear any of their old songs, I can also remember the guy I had a crush on when that song was popular.

—Same here with girls.

—It's amazing how vivid those images are . . .

—I know.

—"Please Please Me" – Ralph Krulder.

—"Eight Days a Week" – Barbara Graber.

—"Yesterday" – Gary Drummond.

—"Michelle" – Nancy Edelman.

—Why would "Michelle" remind you of a girl named Nancy?

—That I don't remember.

—Jesus, you're odd.

—It was a great time though, you know? I remember I was in eighth grade when they first came to the United States, it was like in February or March, and the timing was perfect because it got the whole country excited and it helped get us out of the depression everyone was in since Kennedy was shot that past November.

—I never thought of it that way, but you're probably right. Were you one of those guys who stood in front of the mirror and pretended you were a Beatle?

—Oh, sure.

—So did my brother.

—I would comb my hair forward and either sing along to one of their songs or conduct my own press conference.

—Your own press conference?

—Oh, yeah. I would field questions about my impressions of the United States or about how John was the married one and then I would dash out of my parents' house and wave to the neighbors as I walked very quickly to our station wagon which I made believe was an awaiting limo.

—Jesus, you're odd . . .

— . . . Gilbert?

—Yeah?

—Are the people still singing outside?

—Yeah. "Imagine."

—You know, I can understand it being haunting if you're inside that building. But I, myself, also feel the need to be with other people our age who lived through everything we did.

—I know. But you know what I'm thinking about now?

—What, Gilbert?

—That at this time last night, John Lennon was alive.

—Yeah . . .

—And this morning, and when I passed him in the courtyard this afternoon, and even three hours ago – he was living his life and making his music and being a father and he had no clue whatsoever it would all end tonight.

—I think about that stuff a lot. You know, like, if I had the choice, whether or not I'd want to know exactly when I'm going to die.

—And . . . ?

—I'm not sure. It keeps changing. On one hand, I don't want to know. Let it just happen when it's meant to happen and that will be it. But then, on the other hand, I think there's some value to . . .

—Ten minutes.

—What?

—I've thought a lot about this, too, Zweibel. Don't forget that I watched my dad die a slow death, and no one should have to go through the process of clinging to hope and then giving in to the horror of knowing the end is near.

—So what's this "ten minutes" business?

—It's a compromise. Let me live my life. Let me do what I do. And then, ten minutes before I'm supposed to die, God should let me know so I can make a few phone calls and maybe wolf down a couple of cheeseburgers.

—Ten minutes?

—Yep.

—Not bad, Gilbert.

—Plus . . .

—Oh, there's a bonus?

—Uh-huh . . .

—Yay . . .

—Plus, you get to ask God a question.

—What do you mean?

—Look, you're about to die anyway, right? So, as part of the deal, just before your eyes close for the last time – so even *you* couldn't blabber it to everyone – you get to ask God any question that's been bugging you like, "Who killed Kennedy?" or "Where is Hoffa buried?" You know, questions like that.

—Sure.

—Not a bad idea, huh?

—It's a great idea. Do you know what you would ask him?

—Probably the Kennedy question. That whole thing's always fascinated me so I'd really like to find out the truth about it once and for all.

—I understand.

—What about you, Zweibel?

—What would I ask God?

—Uh-huh.

—And you only get one question?

—Only one question.

— . . . Avocado pits. Why did he make them so big? They take up all that space inside the avocado and it's dumb and it's disproportionate and I want to know what he was thinking when he designed it that way.

—That's what you would ask him?

—Uh-huh.

—You get one question about anything in life and you're going to ask about the size of avocado pits?

—Why not?

—You're an idiot.

—Why?

—Because it's a waste of a question.

—Oh, is that so?

—Yes, that's so.

—And do you know the answer?

—No.

—Then why's it a waste?

—Come on . . .

—Oh, like your Kennedy question isn't a waste.

—It isn't.

—Oh, like you're not going to find out the answer the minute you get to heaven and see J. Edgar Hoover giggling.

— . . . Zweibel?

—Yeah?

—I'm starting to get sleepy.

—Okay.

—Thanks for . . .

—Gilbert?

—Yeah?

—Can I ask you one very quick question?

— . . . Sure.

—Why didn't you want us to come over tonight?

—I told you . . .

—I know what you told me. But I was just wondering if everything was okay with you guys.

— . . . Sure, I'm having fun being married.

—Great.

—Good night, Zweibel.

—Good night, Gilbert.

Long Distance – Six Months Later

—I can't believe I'm a father.

—I'm proud of you.

—I can't believe it. I can't believe that I had sex and actually have something to show for it.

—A son named Adam.

—How do you know his name?

—Robin told me.

—You spoke to her?

—Yeah. When I got your message I called the hospital and Robin told me she was feeling great and that the baby is beautiful and that you had just left to go home and lie down because ultimately you ended up having a much tougher labor than she did.

—Did she tell you what went on in that waiting room?

—Between her parents and yours?

—It was insane.

—She told me.

—Gilda, these are people who hadn't seen or even spoken to each other since my wedding two years ago . . .

—I know . . .

—Until yesterday, when, like sharks moving in for the kill, all four of them descended upon the hospital's waiting room for the final phase of the "Your Baby Should Be Named After *Our Dead Relative*" sweepstakes.

—It's unbelievable. Robin said they've actually been offering you bribes . . . ?

—Oh, yeah . . .

— . . . and that on any given morning you'd open your mail and find the name "Murray" with a ten-dollar bill wrapped around it . . . ?

—Oh, yeah . . .

—Jesus . . .

—"Isaac" went for fifty . . .

—This is an amazing tale.

—I know. But it was the hospital stuff that really made me nuts. Twenty-six hours, Gilda. For twenty-six straight hours I was doing Lamaze in one room, and then, between contractions, running over to the waiting room where they wore me down so much that at one point I actually gave very serious thought to naming the baby "Grandpa" so they'd all be happy and shut the hell up.

—So who was Adam named after?

—No one in particular. Robin and I just liked the name.

—So how did you handle . . . ?

—I gave both sets of parents back all the money they sent us and privately told each of them that Adam's circumcision could take place at their house.

—But . . .

—Don't worry, I'll think of something.

— . . . Zweibel?

—Yeah?

—Was it great? The baby-being-born part? Was it as great as everyone says it is?

—It was the most amazing experience I've ever had in my life. Every cliché I've ever heard about it is absolutely true. When that baby comes out, you can't help but cry and feel that you've just been a part of a miracle and that all of your troubles will somehow magically go away.

—That's wonderful . . .

—And how are you doing, Gilbert?

—Real good.

—The movie's going well?

—Yeah. We're still here in Arizona . . .

—Uh-huh . . .

—And Gene's real funny to work with.

—Uh-huh . . .

—You like him, Zweibel?

—Oh, sure. He made me laugh a lot in *The Producers* and in *Blazing Saddles* and, what was the name of the movie where he played that rabbi who was traveling cross-country and he . . . ?

—*The Frisco Kid.*

—Yeah, that's the one.

—So you like him?

—I like his work very much.

—And how about as a person?

—What do you mean, Gilda?

—Do you like Gene as a person?

—I don't know.

—What do you mean?

—I never met Gene as a person.

—Oh. But if you did meet him, do you think you'd like him as a person?

—Gilda . . . ?

—What?

—Am I going to meet Gene as a person?

—Yes.

In Central Park – Two Weeks Later

—I don't get it, Gilda.

—What don't you get?

—I don't know. I guess I was just under the impression that you guys loved each other and that your marriage was going good.

—Well, in a way we still do love each other, but the two of us have so many of the same needs that the marriage really wasn't working at all.

—You mean like you both need to be with somebody stronger than each other?

—Exactly.

—I understand . . .

—Like you and Robin.

—What do you mean?

—I mean that, on one hand, there's Robin, who's this strong, practical, sensible girl . . .

—Yeah . . . ?

— . . . and on the other hand . . .

—Yeah . . . ?

—There's you.

—I understand.

—You know what I mean, Zweibel?

—Yeah, yeah, yeah, I know what you mean.

—It's not like it's a bad thing.

—No, it's a wonderful thing.

—It's just that that's the way it is. But that's exactly why things didn't work out for me.

—But now you and Gene . . .

—Do you like him?

—As a person?

—Yeah. Now that you've met him and actually have had a delicious dinner with him?

—Well, we thought he was great . . .

—Thank you.

— . . . and that the two of you looked extremely happy eating Japanese food together . . .

—Thank you.

—But I still don't understand why you're moving to Los Angeles.

—Because I want to start a new life where I'm with someone who wants to be with me for no reason other than he loves me. And since Gene and I enjoy working together, I can have both my personal life and my professional life under the same roof.

—But we have roofs here on the East Coast . . .

—Zweibel . . .

—Lots of roofs. I've seen them.

—Zweibel . . .

—What?

—Please be happy for me.

—I am.

—Look, I'm going to miss you, too, but I really don't want to go through the rest of my life just being "Aunt Gilda" to other people's kids. I have to move on.

—I understand.

—Thanks . . .

—And just know that this secret about you getting divorced and moving in with Gene is more than safe with me. Can I tell Robin, though?

—Robin already knows.

—She does?

—Yeah.

—How did she find out?

—I told her.

—Oh . . . when?

—A few days ago.

—Oh . . .

—I told her not to say anything. I wanted to tell you myself.

—So, let me see if I understand this correctly. Last night . . .

—Yeah . . . ?

— . . . when you, me, Robin and Gene were in the restaurant eating our delicious Japanese dinner . . .

—Uh-huh . . .

— . . . I was the only one who had no clue about what was going on?

—You mean between me and Gene?

—That's right.

—Well, yeah . . .

—So that means that when the four of us were sitting there talking about divorces and attorneys I was the only one who thought it was just a figure of speech?

—I guess so.

—You know something, Gilbert?

—What?

—Maybe you've been right all along. Maybe I am an idiot.

At Her Dinner Party – Six Months Later

—Things are different, aren't they, Zweibel?

—Between you and me?

—Yeah.

—Well, I guess it's bound to be a little awkward since we don't see each other for months at a time now.

—I suppose so.

—But I'm happy for you, Gilbert. You're doing good.

—You really think so?

—Hey, look at you. You look beautiful. New clothes, new hairdo, new tan, new friends . . .

—New husband.

—What?

—Gene and I are getting married.

—That's great.

—Thanks.

—When?

—This summer.

—Here in L.A.?

—No.

—Back East?

—France.

—France is east.

—Gene knows a little town in the South of France that's really beautiful, so we're going to have a private ceremony and do some traveling and then get back here in time to prepare for the movie we start shooting in October.

—Wow.

—That is, unless I get pregnant first . . .

—Jesus, Gilda, you're doing it. You're actually putting your whole life together the way you said you were going to.

—It's been a long haul. But I think it's starting to happen.

—I'll say.

—And how are things with you?

—They're coming along.

—Robin told me about your play . . .

—Uh-huh . . .

—And about the meetings with the studios you're out here for.

—Yeah, things are starting to fall into place.

—And Adam?

—He's great.

—Look how your face just lit up.

—Well, he's nine months old and he's just an extraordinary center fielder.

—Oh, really?

—Trust me. I know baseball.

—I know you do. Whose parents is he staying with while you and Robin are out here?

—No one's.

—What do you mean?

—Well, I really didn't think that Adam's limbs could withstand another grandparental tug-of-war, so, as far as all of them are concerned, we brought Adam out here with us.

—But where is he really?

—In New York with Robin's sister.

—Carole?

—Yep. And the few times that our parents have called us at the hotel, we've played a tape of Adam crying in the background.

—You do not.

—Ask Robin. She carries the cassette in her pocketbook in case we're ever paged in a restaurant.

—God . . .

—What?

—You guys make parenthood seem like a real adventure.

—It is. It's a lot of fun.

—Is it?

—You'll see.

Two Years Later

—It's a girl!

—Oh, that's great!

—A beautiful little girl . . .

—Congratulations, Zweibel.

—Thanks.

—How's Robin doing?

—Fine.

—Good.

—The labor was much shorter than it was with Adam and a lot less painful since our parents didn't show up at the hospital.

—This is so exciting.

—I know . . .

—Does the baby have a name yet?

—Lindsay.

—That's so pretty.

—Yeah, she's a great mayor. Remember her grace under pressure during the transit strike?

—Okay, okay . . .

—Sorry.

—Now, Zweibel . . . ?

—Yeah?

—How long does Robin have to stay in the hospital for?

—Um . . .

—Because I want to send her something.

—She's home.

—Robin's home already?

—Yeah.

—Zweibel . . .

—What?

—When was Lindsay born?

— . . . Tuesday.

—Tuesday?

—Yeah . . .

—That's three days ago.

—Well, things have been real hectic and I've been doing a lot of running around and . . .

—You cocksucker!

—Hey . . .

—I know exactly why you waited three days to tell me, you spineless son of a bitch!

—Gilda . . .

—Just like I know why every time we spoke on the phone you never mentioned the pregnancy, or even Adam, unless I brought it up first. You feel sorry for me.

—No I don't.

—Yes you do, and I hate you for it! Don't you know by now that one thing has nothing to do with the other? That I can be happy about you and your family even though I'm having trouble getting pregnant myself?

—Look, Gilda, I know how much it means to you and how hard you're trying and all those tests you're taking . . .

—So? What do you think happens? That when we talk about your children I cry myself to sleep once we get off the phone?

—No . . .

—I don't want your fucking sympathy. You hear me? That's not what our relationship was ever about.

—Look, I just didn't want to be insensitive. But I'm sorry if I didn't handle it well.

—You handled it like a shit.

Peace Talks

—Hello?

—Robin said we should talk.

—Hi, Zweibel.

—She said you weren't feeling well.

—And she told me that you don't believe it.

—Look, Gilda, all I know is that I was out there in Los Angeles for close to two months doing that pilot and we didn't see each other even once.

—I know . . .

—We made all these lunch plans and dinner plans and we were even supposed to go to that movie premiere and I'm supposed to be the one who's the flake but you're the one who broke those dates every single time.

—Look, Zweibel . . .

—So what am I supposed to think? That you're still mad at me for not calling you when Lindsay was born?

—No . . .

—Or for what I said about Gene's and your last movie?

—What did you say about our last movie?

—Oh . . . ah . . . nothing.

—Look, the truth is I *haven't* been feeling well.

—For two months, Gilda?

—Actually, it's been going on a little longer than that.

—What's wrong with you?

—I have no strength. And I'm tired all of the time. I swear to you, Zweibel, every time you and I made plans I really wanted to see you, but then I ended up going to bed early or going to some doctor and that's what my whole life's been lately.

—And what do the doctors say?

—That I have Epstein-Barr virus.

—Oh . . .

—You've heard of it?

—Yeah, it's like mono, right?

—It's horrible. My mind wants to do everything I always do but my body's just too tired to do it.

—And how long does this virus last for?

—Well, it depends on which doctor you listen to . . .

—Do you have faith in these guys, Gilbert?

—I guess so.

—You guess so?

—I mean, they all say the same thing, you know, that I have EBV . . .

—Uh-huh . . .

— . . . but I've decided to believe the doctors who say that this will be over soon because I'm getting pissed off at not feeling good.

—I can understand that.

—Real pissed off.

—Look, honey, I'm sorry if I misread the situation.

—You wouldn't be you if you didn't.

—It's just that I miss you and . . .

—When are you coming out here again?

—Well, if this pilot I did becomes a series, I'll be out there again in about a month to start hiring a staff.

—A month?

—Yeah . . .

—I'll be better by then.

—Well, you just take it easy and do what the doctors say and . . .

—Zweibel . . .

—What?

—Call me when you know for sure when you're coming out.

—Okay . . .

—And we'll go out and play.

—Okay, Gilda.

—And Zweibel?

—Yeah?

—Gene's and my last movie . . . ?

—Yeah?

—Sucked.

In a Rented House —
A Month Later

—Hello?

—Hi, Zweibel.

—Hey, Gilbert. What a great surprise. How'd you get this number? This phone was put in only about an hour ago.

—I called Robin in New York and she gave it to me.

—And did she tell you who I'm renting this house from?

—Larry Fine, right?

—Yep, from the Three Stooges. The doorbell rang before and I was afraid to answer it because I was positive that the guy from Federal Express was going to poke me in the eyes and hit me over the head with my package.

—Now how long are you out here for?

—Well, the network ordered six episodes of the show . . .

—I know, congratulations.

—So Garry and I are going to write and produce them and that will take a few months.

—I see.

—And even though I'll be flying back East to be with Robin

and the kids on the weekends, there'll still be plenty of time for you and me to get together whenever you feel up to it.

—Good.

—No pressure, and I promise I won't get mad if you have to break . . .

—No, I really want to see you.

—Great. So you're feeling better?

—Zweibel . . . ?

—Yeah?

—I just found out that I don't have Epstein-Barr virus.

—Hey, that's great!

—I have cancer.

— . . . Gilda?

—I have ovarian cancer, Zweibel, and I need you to help me get through this part of my life.

— . . . I will.

—You promise?

—I promise. What should I do first?

—Make me laugh.

In a Restaurant

—Your new show is really funny.

—Thanks, Gilbert.

—And it's fun reading about you in all the great reviews you guys are getting.

—I memorized all those great reviews. You want to hear?

—No, that's okay.

—Sure?

—Quite. Now tell me about Garry. What's he like?

—He's a good guy.

—And you enjoy working with him?

—Very much. We think alike, so writing together has been a lot of fun.

—And does he know what kind of pain in the ass you can be if he doesn't deliver your lines exactly the way you want him to?

—No, Gilda, and I'd appreciate it if you didn't tell him.

—I won't.

—I say let him find out on his own . . .

—Like I did.

—Exactly.

—Poor Garry.

—I know . . . Gilda?

—Yeah?

—How are you feeling?

—Annoyed. Like all of a sudden I've become a member in an elite club that I'd rather not belong to. But it's Gene that I really feel bad for. He's going through hell.

At the Zoo

—You know what happened at the Laker game, Zweibel?

—What?

—We were in these courtside seats, and during the warm-ups, Kareem recognized me even though I was wearing the same kerchief I'm wearing now. So he walked up to me, pointed to his bald head, smiled and said, "Don't worry, Gilda. I'll get you a pair of goggles and you'll be just fine." I like Kareem. He's a good guy.

On the Phone

—Hello?

—Gilda, are you okay?

—Yeah . . .

—I called you a thousand times last night.

—I know.

—How do you know? I didn't leave any messages on your machine . . .

—I know.

— . . . because I thought it would be a big pain in your ass to come home and hear that the same person called a thousand times.

—That's very considerate of you.

—Well, you know . . .

—So, instead, you figured it would be a lot more exciting for me to come home and listen to someone hang up on my machine a thousand times.

—Yes.

—Thank you.

—So, where were you last night?

—I was home.

—I mean when I was calling you all those times.

—I was home.

—Then why didn't you answer the phone?

—Because I was trying to work.

—On what?

—I was writing.

—Really?

—Yes.

—Wow . . . That's great, Gilda . . . What were you writing?

—A book.

—Wow . . . That's great . . . What kind of book?

—An autobiography.

—So it's a book about you.

—It's about me and my life and, who knows, maybe I can help some people by writing about what I'm going through right now.

—That sounds great.

—Well, it's hard work. I don't have to tell you how difficult being alone in a room and writing can be . . .

—You can do it, though.

—I hope so.

—Sure you can, Gilbert.

—We'll see.

—You just have to concentrate . . .

—I know . . .

— . . . and try to block out all distractions.

—Tell me about it.

—Gilda . . . ?

—Yes?

—Am I in your book?

—Do you mean do I mention you in my book?

—Mention, describe, go on and on and on in vivid detail about . . .

—Yes, you pain in the ass, you're in the book.

—Really? . . . I'm honored . . . How many times?

—So far, once.

—Uh-huh . . . And what page are you on?

—Page 54.

—And, uh, any idea how many pages this book ultimately might be?

—Well, I told the publisher that it would end up being around two hundred and fifty pages.

—Uh-huh. So, at this "one mention per fifty pages" rate, it's not inconceivable that my name could be . . .

—Ripped out of my typewriter and shoved straight up your ass if you don't stop bugging me? Yes.

—You know something, honey? Maybe we should hang up so you could continue with your work.

—Good idea.

—Write away, kid.

—Jesus.

In Her Backyard

—You look tired, Zweibel.

—Thanks, I *feel* pretty good.

—I said you look tired, you idiot.

—Oh. Well, I am tired. I've been putting in some incredibly long hours at the show.

—I know.

—Plus, these weekend trips back and forth across the country are starting to take their toll on me. Every Friday night it's the red-eye to New York, and then Monday mornings I take the 7:00 flight to get back here. I swear to you, Gilda, I can't even remember the last time I went to the bathroom twice in a row in the same time zone.

—But isn't that all going to change soon? Robin told me that since your show's been picked up for at least another season, you're thinking of moving the family out here.

—Yeah, Robin's going to fly out next week and we'll try to rent a house in Brentwood in time for Adam to start school in September.

—Brentwood's beautiful . . .

—Yeah, it's got nice neighborhoods and lots of trees.

—Santa Monica's pretty, too.

—I know, but we can't live there.

—Why not?

—Because we figured out that Santa Monica is a few miles closer to Long Island than it is to New Jersey and that could cause problems with Robin's parents.

—Oh, I forgot. Which reminds me, your mom called me.

—She asked if it would be okay and I told her that I thought you'd appreciate it.

—She was real sweet.

—Oh, good.

—And then she spent an hour and a half telling me how she and your dad had to change temples when you embarrassed her old rabbi by putting his name on TV in a speech about men who drool into their beards.

—Oh, God . . .

—But she was real funny and she made me laugh a lot.

—Oh, good . . .

—Now, Zweibel . . . ?

—Yeah?

—Can we talk about your show?

—Sure . . .

—And me being on it?

—Sure.

—Do you think I should do it?

—It's entirely up to you, Gilbert. I think it would be a lot of fun working with you again, and you and Garry could be real funny together.

—I really like Garry.

—He's crazy about you, too. But if you're not feeling up to it or if you'd rather not . . .

—I'm nervous, Zweibel. I haven't worked in a long time and I'm afraid that no one in your audience is even going to know who I am.

—I wouldn't worry about that, Gilbert. Everyone is going to . . .

—But then, on the other hand, I want to do it more than anything. I'm tired of being sick and I want to fight this fucker. And I've only got one weapon. And I've got to use it. So I guess I do want to do your show. I want you to help me make cancer funny.

Thoughts While Pacing a Studio Floor

—This feeling. God, I remember this feeling. Garry's standing there delivering some monologue about sea monkeys but I don't hear a word he's saying because Gilda's on the other side of the door to his TV apartment waiting to walk onto the set as a surprise to this unsuspecting audience.

GARRY
... and sea monkeys make great pets. Look
at this one here. I think he recognizes me.
Hi, fella ...

—This feeling's been creeping up on me all week, as if an old song was playing and I was reliving what I felt back then. Gilda's walk entering a rehearsal hall. Gilda's voice saying words that I've written. Gilda's voice changing words that I've written. Gilda laughing as a 300-pound cameraman gives her a piggyback ride around the studio.

> GARRY
>
> Boy, this one looks tough. I'm going to call him
> Buster. Sea monkeys are very protective. Sick
> 'em, Buster . . .

—The differences are haunting, though. Food picked at but not eaten. Naps in a dressing room between scenes. And the eerie frustration of getting her answering machine, which, with each passing night, seems to be turned on earlier.

> GARRY
>
> You know, when Columbus discovered America,
> he also discovered sea monkeys and . . .

There's a knock at the door.

> GARRY
>
> . . . I wonder who that is.

Garry walks to the front door and opens it.

> GILDA
>
> Hi, Garry.

> GARRY
>
> Hi, Gilda.
> (*to the audience*)
> Hey, everybody – it's Gilda!

—My God. Look at her. Look at Gilda. All she's said so far is "Hi, Garry," but look at what's happening in this studio. Look how you can feel the connection between 250 strangers with someone who didn't know if anyone would remember. Look at them standing. Clapping. Cheering. Look at her face. She's smiling. And look at their faces. A lot of them, including the 300-pound cameraman, are crying.

Century City Hospital

—Mr. Zweibel?

—Yes.

—How do you do? I'm Kathy.

—Hi, Kathy.

—Are you comfortable?

—Sure.

—Have you ever given blood before?

—Yes.

—Very good. So, what do you say we get started?

—What's this, Kathy?

—Excuse me?

—Why'd you just hand me this pen and paper?

—Oh, Gilda likes it when people write her notes which we tape to the pouch so she can think of that person during her transfusion.

—Oh, okay . . .

—Is Gilda a friend of yours?

—Yes.

—Write something nice. She's having a tough time and we're pretty crazy about her around here.

A Note
on a Transfusion Bottle

Dear Gilbert,

I knew I'd finally get some fluid of mine into you one way or another.

Love,
Zweibel

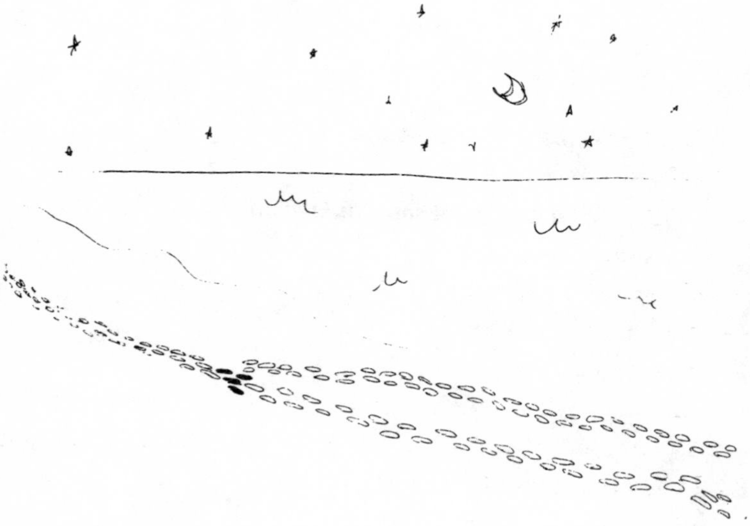

A Walk on a Beach

—The ocean looks peaceful tonight.

—Yeah, it does.

—And look how pretty the moon is.

— . . . Gilda?

—Yeah?

—I read your book.

—You did?

—Yeah, last night I had the house to myself because Robin and the kids are back East. So I made a fire and sat in the den and read your manuscript.

—And . . . ?

—I think it's wonderful.

—Really?

—Yeah, Gilda. It's great.

—Thanks . . .

—I don't know how to handle a lot of it, though.

—What do you mean?

—I . . . I didn't know about a lot of the stuff you've been going through. Some of the procedures, and the pain . . . I wish I had known.

—And you would've done what about it?

—I don't know, but . . .

—That was never part of our deal, Zweibel. Remember?

—Yeah . . .

—Hey, my doctors really laughed when they saw the note you wrote me.

—They did?

—Except for one doctor who didn't understand the history of our relationship. So I tried my best to explain it to him . . .

—Yeah . . . ?

— . . . and then *I* got confused.

—What's there to be confused about? You always said we should take things slowly and we are.

—Zweibel?

—Yeah?

—If I ask you a question, do you promise to take it the right way?

—Sure . . .

—Because I know how happy you are with Robin . . .

—Right . . .

—And I'm real happy with Gene . . .

—Right . . .

—But, how come we never got married?

—I've thought about that, Gilda.

—You have?

—Oh, yeah . . .

—And . . . ?

—I think we just forgot to.

—We forgot to get married?

—It's the best conclusion I can come up with . . . Hey, are you okay?

—Can you do me a favor, Zweibel?

—What?

—Put your arm around me?

—Cold?

—A little.

—Want to head back to the car?

—No, let's keep walking.

— . . . Okay.

Two Months Later

—Alan . . . ?

—Huh?

—The phone.

—What, Robin?

—The phone's ringing.

—Who the hell . . . ?

—It's probably your mother calling to wish you a happy birth-day.

—At six in the morning?

—Alan, she still gets confused whether she should add or subtract three hours when she compares our time to New York's.

—Jesus . . .

—I'm telling you, Alan, she thinks it's noon.

—Okay, hand me the phone.

—Here . . .

—*Hello . . . Yes, this is Alan . . . Oh, no . . .*

At a Memorial — June 1, 1989

—About fourteen years ago I was hiding behind a potted plant and this girl asked if I could help her be a parakeet, and I've been smitten with Gilda ever since. When we met, we were just these two kids in a big city and, because we made each other laugh, people invited us places we never got to go before. And now? Well, I haven't mourned, and I haven't even cried yet, because even though she's dead, I just don't want her to die. I don't know why God makes people and then takes them back while they're still having fun with the life he gave them in the first place. Just like I don't know if I'm supposed to celebrate the fact that Gilda was in my life, or feel cheated that she's not here anymore. But even though her body grew to betray her, spirits just don't die. And that's what Gilda was. Even as an adult, she was still a little girl who believed in fairy tales and that if she said "Bunny Bunny" on the first day of every month, it would bring her love, laughter and peace. Well, Gilda, this is June 1st and if you're in a place where you can't say it, I'll say it for you—"Bunny Bunny" and I hope you're okay. I'm gonna miss you, Gilbert.

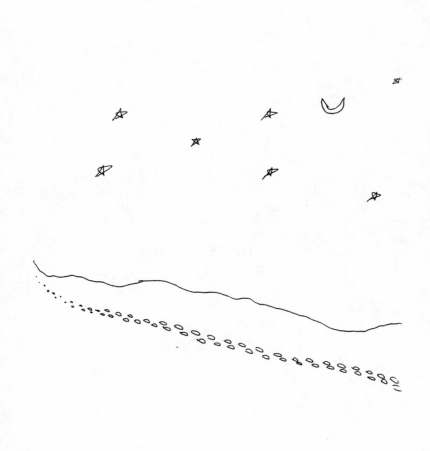

About the Author

ALAN ZWEIBEL has received numerous writing awards for his work in television, which includes *Saturday Night Live* and PBS's *Great Performances,* as well as *It's Garry Shandling's Show* and *The Canterberrys' Tales* (both of which he cocreated and produced). And even though his plays *Between Cars* and *Comic Dialogue* enjoyed critically acclaimed off-Broadway runs; and his fiction has appeared in such diverse publications as *Mad* magazine and *The Atlantic;* and he cowrote the screenplay for Rob Reiner's film *North,* which he adapted from his own novel, Zweibel still wishes that he had more credits so there wouldn't be so many blank pages at the end of this book.

Alan and his wife, Robin, live in Los Angeles and New Jersey with their children, Adam, Lindsay, and Sari.